Today Is Tomorrow

Today Is Tomorrow

Assessing Today's K–12 Education for Success in the Future

M. Scott Norton

ROWMAN & LITTLEFIELD
Lanham • Boulder • New York • London

Published by Rowman & Littlefield
An imprint of The Rowman & Littlefield Publishing Group, Inc.
4501 Forbes Boulevard, Suite 200, Lanham, Maryland 20706
https://rowman.com

6 Tinworth Street, London SE11 5AL, United Kingdom

Copyright © 2020 by M. Scott Norton

All rights reserved. No part of this book may be reproduced in any form or by any electronic or mechanical means, including information storage and retrieval systems, without written permission from the publisher, except by a reviewer who may quote passages in a review.

British Library Cataloguing in Publication Information Available

Library of Congress Cataloging-in-Publication Data

Library of Congress Control Number: 2019951681
ISBN 978-1-4758-5231-8 (cloth)
ISBN 978-1-4758-5232-5 (pbk.)
ISBN 978-1-4758-5233-2 (Electronic)

Contents

Preface	ix
Why This Book Was Written	ix
How This Book Is Organized	x

1 Public School Education in America: Patchwork or a Complete Makeover?   1
- Primary Chapter Goal   1
- The Status of K–12 Education in America   1
- Not Melodrama and Magical Thinking   2
- The Critical Failures of Public Education   3
- Major Factors That Are Inhibiting Public School Quality   4
- A Lightbulb Experience   7
- Organizational Development and School Improvement   11
- The Major Success Factors of Public Education: The Other Side of the Story   12
- Nevertheless, the Criticism of Public Education Remains with Us   16
- Post-Chapter Quiz   17
- Post-Quiz, True or False   20
- Discussion of the Post-Chapter Quiz   21
- Answers to the True or False Post-Quiz   24
- Thoughts on What Is Right with Public Education   25
- Key Chapter Ideas and Recommendations   25
- Discussion Questions   27
- Case Study   28
- References   28

2 Education Futurology Based on Current Trends and Conditions   31
- Primary Chapter Goal   31

	Your Guess Is as Good as Mine	31
	Is Oral and Written Communication Going Away?	32
	Critical Thinking and Students' Effectiveness	32
	Old Wine in Old Bottles	33
	New Wine in New Bottles	35
	Critical Thinking and Decision-Making: Two Intertwined Entities	36
	Group Decision-Making Strategies	37
	Gaining New Ideas from Brainstorming	39
	Decision-Making and Educational Administration	40
	A Look at Probable Changes in Educational Practices	41
	Education's Missing Link: Quality Research Practices	41
	What Is Needed to Help Make Education in America the Best in the World?	42
	Major Success Factors of Public Education That Need to Be Extended	45
	High School Graduation Statistics	46
	Post-Chapter Quiz/Review	47
	Answers to the Chapter's Post-Quiz	48
	Key Chapter Ideas and Recommendations	50
	Discussion Questions	51
	References	52
3	K–12 Education and the Future	53
	Primary Chapter Goal	53
	Predicting the Future	53
	Future Projections: School Building Construction	55
	What about Education, the School's Curriculum, and the Classrooms in 2030?	57
	The 2030 Curriculum in the Nowalls School District in Lafayette	58
	What about Program Subject Content for Education in the Future?	60
	How the Contemporary Skills Are Developed in K–12 Education Programs	61
	Serving Students by Fostering Skill Sets That Prepare Them for the Future	62
	What Does It Take to Have Effective Collaboration?	63
	What Is Often Overlooked? A Snapshot of the Small Stuff	64
	Failure Is Acceptable or Is It?	65
	Failure as a Positive Happening	65
	A Lighthouse Experience: Education Technology	67
	The Three Ts of Today's Educational Technology	67
	New Terms, New Knowledge, and New Understandings	68
	A Chapter Post-Quiz	73
	Answers to the Chapter Post-Quiz	74

	Key Chapter Ideas and Recommendations	75
	Discussion Questions	77
	References	77
4	Education Today for Meeting the Challenges of Tomorrow	79
	Primary Chapter Goal	79
	Educational Success Today and Educational Success Tomorrow	79
	Social Science Looms High among Projected Future Skills	80
	Social Skills Can be Learned, Observed, and Practiced	81
	The Importance of Affective Skills	81
	The Enhancement of Social Skills	84
	The Social Skill of Mentoring: Old Wine in New Bottles	84
	The Characteristic of Adaptability: An Essential Skill in a Changing World	86
	Attention to Details: A Skill of Paramount Importance for Future Success	87
	Helping Students Develop the Skill of Being Attentive to Details	88
	Negotiations as a Positive Activity: Are You Serious?	89
	Negotiations Will Continue to Be a Part of Our Everyday Life	89
	Service Orientation and Future Success	90
	The Important Quality of Coordination	92
	Technology and Future Student Success	93
	Post-Quiz for Chapter 4	94
	Answers to the Post-Quiz	97
	Your Post-Quiz Results	98
	Key Chapter Ideas and Recommendations	99
	Action Activities	99
	References	100

About the Author   101

Preface

WHY THIS BOOK WAS WRITTEN

Differences concerning the primary purposes of education historically have been expressed. Such differences continue to be "argued." Should K–12 education today serve each and every child by giving them the knowledge and skills they will need for participating successfully in the future? Although considerable support is expressed for this major goal, a great deal of thought is given to the belief that today's success is what should be the primary concern of student education. Live for today since no one can predict what their future might bring.

The title of this book, *Today Is Tomorrow,* does carry considerable truth. Many of the stated purposes of contemporary education also appear in the projections for the future of education as well. In order to help clarify the matter of education today and success in the future, available literature on the topic, projections for America's future in the next several decades were examined and assessed. Not only were the implications for expected change in communication technology and computer-related developments given much attention, but the social environment in the year 2030 and beyond were investigated. The reader will find the findings related to social changes of great interest.

In the study of a projected future for education, we contend that "logical" projections for the future have important implications as to the goals and objectives of K–12 education in today's school programs. Answering the questions related to a projected future and the importance of serving students for today and for tomorrow is why this book was written. We believe that the reader will become engaged in the book's contents and somewhat intrigued by the relationship of today's school program purposes and the projected "photo" of successful living in the world of tomorrow.

HOW THIS BOOK IS ORGANIZED

The book includes four chapters that include an in-depth discussion of education in America today and logical projections of expected changes in the internal and external environments of education in the years ahead. Chapter 1 examines today's education in America in terms of its "failures" that have inhibited program effectiveness. Such important program matters as organizational development needs are discussed along with the success factors that have been evidenced in school programs over the years.

Chapter 2 centers on futurology that is based on current trends and conditions. Such characteristics as critical thinking and student effectiveness, group decision-making and educational administration, the need for quality research provisions within the school program are discussed. The question "What is needed to make education the best in the world?" is addressed. Major success factors that need to be expanded in education are recommended.

Chapter 3 centers on education and the future. Future projections related to school building construction, curriculum and subject-matter curriculum are given primary attention. How contemporary knowledge and skills are developed is given primary consideration. Such characteristics as extended collaboration and other skills that serve to prepare students for the future are discussed. At one point in the chapter, the topic of failure as a positive happening is an interesting reading. Failure is a factor in some way in most everyone's life. How can one benefit when failure does occur?

Chapter 4 centers on the question of how today's education can serve to meet the challenges for tomorrow. Social science, somewhat surprisingly, looms high among the projected future skills of importance. Adaptability, attention to details, positive negotiations, service orientation, coordination, and technology are presented for their importance in meeting future needs.

Chapter 4, as well as the other book chapters, contain a section of key ideas and recommendations, discussion questions, and chapter references for extended reading. This book will prove to be of special interest and value to any practicing educator. In addition, parents and educators in higher education will find the book of special interest. We contend that any citizen who has special interest in K–12 education and education for the future will enjoy the contents of this book. Lastly, each reader will have a better understanding of education's purposes and the relationship of today's school programming and children's future success.

Chapter One

Public School Education in America

Patchwork or a Complete Makeover?

PRIMARY CHAPTER GOAL

To examine the wide division of views relative to the current effectiveness of public school education in America and the major reasons why educational reforms seldom result in long-term improvements, wide public acceptance, or equity for learners nationwide.

THE STATUS OF K–12 EDUCATION IN AMERICA

In an article set forth by McSpadden (2015), the primary contention was that public schools in America are doing very well. In fact, in schools with less than 25 percent poverty rates, American children scored higher in reading than any children in other countries. Yet, in 2014, reports indicated that latest international ratings of education in sixty-five countries showed that public schools in America are in a freefall (Fedewa, 2014); the United States ranked 29th in education in the world.

A few years ago, Sager (2013), contended that the educational system in the United States is in dire trouble and there seemed to be little real hope of effective reform in the near future. He further stated that the educational system has been in a state of decline for decades. Yet, on the other hand, Rampell (2014) cited research that supported the fact that public education is getting better, not worse.

A more recent reference supported public schools and pointed out that public education has gotten a bad rap. Chen (2017) supported Rampell's foregoing contention by pointing out several advantages of public schools including factors such as cost, diversity, academic opportunities, extracurricular opportunities, services, teacher qualifications, and other positive factors. Another source set forth the wide claim that today's schools are better today than at any point in the past (Schneider, 2016). This writer described several indicators that reveal slow but steady improvement in education across many generations. Schneider astutely closes his argument for providing a first-rate public education for every child in America in the paragraph that follows (2016, June 22):

> The evolution of America's school system has been slow. But providing a first-rate public education to every child in the country is a monumental task. Today, 50 million U.S. students attend roughly 100,000 schools, and are educated by over 3 million teachers. The scale alone is overwhelming. And the aim of schooling is equally ambitious. Educators are not just designing gadgets or building websites. At this phenomenal scale, they are trying to make people—a fantastically difficult task for which there is no quick fix. No simple solution, no "hack."
>
> Can policy leaders and stakeholders accelerate the pace of development? Probably. Can the schools do more to realize national ideals around equity and inclusion? Without question. But none of these aims will be achieved by ripping the system apart. That's a ruinous fiction. The struggle to create great schools for all young people demands swift justice and steady effort, not melodrama and magical thinking. (pp. 8–9)

NOT MELODRAMA AND MAGICAL THINKING

The foregoing positions relative to the status of public education, for the most part, are based on personal opinions and perspectives. But is there reliable and valid evidence that reveals the true status of public education in America? Chapter 1 centers on the status of public education as revealed in official status reports of major educational organizations, agencies of the states and federal governments, and other highly reliable sources.

In the following sections of chapter 1, study results rather than public opinions of the pluses and minuses of education are reported. If high-quality school programs can be authenticated, leaders in education can capitalize on such findings. If studies can ferret out what factors are inhibiting public education in America, this information gives leaders a basis for reimagining education with a positive perspective in mind for the future. Chapter 1 centers on six major charges against public education that commonly accompany claims of education's failures and then sets forth five major support factors that are claimed as public education's successes. Identification of positive and negative perspectives of public education are considered, but recommended changes are specifically addressed. Reimagining educational changes are discussed in-depth in chapters 2, 3, and 4.

THE CRITICAL FAILURES OF PUBLIC EDUCATION

Among the myriad of criticisms of public education are the following *inhibiting factors* commonly set forth as failures of public education: (1) lack of financial support including low teachers' salaries; (2) inequities in public school programs across the states; (3) the widening control of education by the states and federal government agencies; (4) the lack of highly qualified teachers and administrator personnel; (5) poor student academic performance that is identified in the list of major factors that result in the failure of public schools; and (6) the "disorganization of schools" including an excessive number of school administrators with overlapping functions, administrative mismanagement, too many inefficient school districts that should be consolidated, and far too many curricular subjects that consume high percentages of the school's budget.

Although the lack of valid and reliable research evidence is not commonly mentioned as an inhibitor of public school success, we contend that it indeed is a missing activity in education. We have taken the factor of "author's privilege" and added it to the list of public school inhibiting factors. Give a moment's thought to the matter of research in educational practices. Can you name a school district that has a quality education research program in operation?

We are not looking at educational research as being the statistical unit for the school district; one in which the student enrollment figures and academic testing programs are reported. Rather, we view the school district's research unit to be one that focuses on the ongoing dissemination of educational research relative to planned pilot programs, active classroom research findings, program findings on topics of educational significance completed by other school districts or agencies, and related research in cooperation with teachers in determining such topics as the learning styles of students in the school.

Each of the inhibiting factors of education is discussed in the following sections of chapter 1. Following that, chapters 2, 3, and 4 focus on the revolutionary changes that must be implemented to overcome these major inhibitors. We begin by discussing the six major inhibitors of public school education as reported within the literature.

MAJOR FACTORS THAT ARE INHIBITING PUBLIC SCHOOL QUALITY

1. Lack of Financial Support as a Primary Inhibitor of Public School Education

Former U.S. president, Richard Nixon, declared that just putting more money into current educational programs will not assure improvements in public education. The contention does hold considerable truth. Giving more money to low-performing school personnel certainly does not assure that teacher performance will improve. However, new money for attracting highly knowledgeable and qualified personnel into education is a much different story. Research evidence has been shown to support the finding that many persons with high intelligence scores are not entering the teaching profession. When they do enter the profession, a large percentage of these talented persons leaves teaching after only one year.

Klein (2011) was straightforward in his contentions for fixing the present education compensation schemes. We paraphrase his comments regarding what should be done to enable the system to meet its financial needs. Rather than paying for longevity and lifetime benefits, Klein contends that we must reward excellence. To do so, automatic raises and promises of large lifetime benefits would have to be eliminated. The enormous amounts of money saved could be devoted to competing for high-quality personnel, differentiated compensation practices, difficult teaching assignment incentives, and successful recruiting in those subject-areas where shortages are in evidence.

In addition, Klein speaks of frontloading compensation whereby new teachers could receive as much as $80,000 within four years of service. Think of how such a provision would serve to attract and retain new highly qualified teacher personnel. The loss of 20 to 30 percent of teachers new to the profession would lessen considerably. Education personnel would receive this frontloading of compensation in the early years of their educational experience. They would not have to wait for twenty-five years or more to "cash in" on the present back-loaded structure. In brief, Klein proposed eliminating the lifetime, defined pensions, monetizing the savings, and then paying it to teachers in their early years. A second alternative was suggested by Rhee that centered on a merit plan whereby teachers could earn higher salaries during their early entry into teaching (Rhee, 2011). We support this "out of the proverbial box" thinking.

The old adage that individuals do not enter teaching for the money, but they do so for the love of children, is flawed. Contemporary teacher strikes such as the *RedforEd 2018* strikes in Arizona are a case in point. The whole purpose of the 2018 Arizona teacher strike was that of salary increases. The state's agreement to increase teachers' salaries 20 percent by 2020 served to resolve the problem for the meantime. Yet, additional teacher demands were soon to follow.

There is sufficient evidence to show that increasingly the classroom teacher is responsible for paying for needed classroom instructional materials. As one teacher pointed out, to do the job that she wants to do, she spends personal funds in the amount that commonly equals the raise that she received for the school year. There appear to be no secrets regarding the importance of funding for recruiting and retaining highly talented teacher personnel. The answers lie in paying teachers what the market demands, providing them with benefits that are competitive, and creating a work environment in which they can derive genuine professional satisfaction.

What Has to Be Done?

Such provisions call for the discontinuance of the single salary schedule whereby all teachers with the same degree and years of experience receive the same compensation regardless of the supply and demand principle or differences in professional job performance. Such obvious solutions are not always easy to implement. Educational finance is among the most difficult inhibitors of quality public school education; getting more money for education is viewed by many authorities as the number one problem being encountered.

Sager (2013) contends that in the face of shortfalls and decreased tax revenues, many school systems in the nation have cut their educational programs. Such cuts result in lasting damages to the education of students. Financial cuts are implemented at the expense of educational quality and result in the contention that America's schools are failing. Lack of funding also leads to the unfortunate practices of cutting programs of learning, reduction of the school year, and in some cases, reducing the school week from five days to four. Those parties that contend that money is not the cause of failing education in America are failing themselves to recognize that cuts in financial support mean cuts in student learning. Recommended solutions to school failure and finances are presented in later chapters of the book.

2. The Inhibitor of Educational Inequities among States and School Districts

The Question: Does Variation in Per-Pupil Spending Explain Most of the Variations in School Quality?

For the most part, public school education is viewed as a state responsibility. Within our fifty states, education equity differs widely. In fact, the quality of public education within any one state differs within the many school districts that commonly exist. Richie Bernardo, writing for WalletHub, (2017, July

17), reported on a fifty-state study that compared the quality of public education in the fifty states on twenty-one key measures. Although the report did come up with several measures of education quality, unfortunately no attention apparently was given to the extent to which the highest rated states financially supported public education. That report asked the question, "Does variation in per-pupil spending explain most of the variation in school quality?" but did not answer it.

We referred to the WalletHub study of public school quality rankings which gave the state of Massachusetts the highest quality ranking with the states of New Jersey, Connecticut, New Hampshire, and Vermont next in order of best public schools. The lowest quality of public schools were New Mexico, Mississippi, Arizona, Alaska, and West Virginia. Just how do these state ratings compare with per-pupil expenditures for public education? In a completely different 2018 report published by Concordia University–Portland (Oregon), the following state per-pupil monetary support was determined:

High School Quality State Ranking	Per-Pupil Spending
1st Massachusetts	$15,592
2nd New Jersey	$18, 235
3rd Connecticut	$18,377
4th New Hampshire	$14,697
5th Vermont	$18,039

Low School Quality State Ranking	Per-Pupil Spending
50th New Mexico	$9,792
42nd Mississippi	$8,456
48th Arizona	$7,485
47th Alaska	$20,172
46th West Virginia	$11,359

Other states with per-pupil spending support of $14,697 or more were:

New Hampshire with $14,697, New York with a quality ranking of 20th and per-pupil support of $21,206, Pennsylvania with a quality ranking of 28th and per-pupil support of $14,717, Rhode Island with a quality ranking of 21st and per-pupil support of $15,179, and Wyoming with a quality rating of 18th and per-pupil support of $16,056.

We note, once again, that the two study reports, one for state education quality and the other for per-pupil spending support, were two separate and distinct reports. The comparative information relative to state education quality and state spending is interesting and does reveal some evidence for answering the question posed at the outset of this section: Does variation in per-pupil spending explain most of the variations in school quality? We contend that financial support does provide some insight for answering the question. However, Alaska with its high school spending per-pupil of $20,172 and New York with spending of $21,206 per-pupil ranked 42nd and 20th for school quality respectively. Authorities tend to view these two states as special cases due to several factors such as population differences, territorial differences, professional personnel issues, and other student clientele differences that must be attended in these states.

A LIGHTBULB EXPERIENCE

Kyle Jaeger (2015, July 13) published an "inequalities article" that is pertinent to our consideration of property valuations and educational tax support. Jaeger notes that half of the country's property value comes from only the five states of California, New York, Florida, Texas, and Pennsylvania, respectively. Furthermore, income inequality is a growing problem in America and as the gap between the rich and poor continues to widen, disparities between property values per state will also increase over time.

Only four states are worth more than New York City property-wise, one of which is New York State. It tends to open one's eyes to the matter of inequity when it is noted that the value of some Manhattan neighborhoods on the east upper side, which occupy less than one square mile, have an outstanding $96 billion of housing value. This fact, according to Jaeger, places it above Staten Island and the Bronx as well as above the six other states of New Hampshire, North Dakota, South Dakota, Vermont, Wyoming, and Alaska. As we are well aware, local public school support comes primarily from monies gained through property taxes.

Statistics relative to the financial status of the fifty states have shown that the ability to pay for education differs in a ratio of 6 to 1. That is, the richest states are able to pay six times more for educational services than the poorest states. A related note focuses on the fact that just given equal amounts of monetary support to rich and poor school communities does nothing to adjust the inequities that exist. For example, if $a < b$ then $a + c < b + c$ meaning that if school district "a" has less property valuation for school purposes than school district "b," then just giving the same school monetary support to each school district does not improve the inequity that exists.

3. The Issue of Increasing Loss of Local Control of Public Education

The U.S. Constitution makes no mention of education, but the Tenth Amendment to the constitution does give the responsibilities not set forth in the constitution to the states and its people. Thus, education commonly has been viewed as a federal concern, state responsibility, and local function. As a local function, district school boards have the primary responsibility of providing policies to guide the actions of those to whom it delegates administrative authority. The formulation and adoption of these written policies constitute the primary method by which the board of education exercises its leadership in the operation of the school system (Norton, 2017).

School board policy development, adoption, and implementation have several special benefits for the local school system because: (1) the quality of teaching and learning effectiveness can be improved because the school is administered by the individuals and boards that are most knowledgeable about the school community and its students' interests and needs; (2) the school purposes and policy decisions are determined by representative school board members, the governance process includes a close working relationship with members of the school staff and community; (3) the external control is substantially reduced which facilitates positive decision-making and implementation of meaningful administrative regulations that can be readily applied to programs for student learning; and (4) local development, adoption, and implementation of school policy provides an important opportunity for the involvement of local school personnel and representative school community members to participate in the process. Thus, the adopted policies become the personal product of not only the school board, but the property of teachers, parents, and other persons who served in their development.

Negative effects on public school quality are also found in other external interventions by federal and state agencies and other state and national associations. The federal government has found its program priorities in many various program activities over the years. Vocational education, agricultural programs, physical education interventions, math, science, special student needs programs, foreign language requirements, and other curricular subjects have found their way into public school programs over the years by federal authorities. Teaching content and methodology were required by federal agencies under the Common Core mandates accompanied by a major increase in student testing measures that served to control public school program operations. Each mandated program was accompanied by federal monies that controlled local curricular operations.

In most every state, school board policies are developed by the state's school board association. Thus, in most every state, every school district has the same policies and administrative regulations using the alpha system for codification purposes. In the foregoing chapter discussion of the benefits of effective school governance policies, we underscored the importance of local school district involvement in the policy development process. When a state's school board association develops the policies for the school district, local control of the school's program is severely threatened and the importance of participative involvement in the process is disregarded. As a result, a school district's policy manuals lay dormant on shelves in teachers' classrooms gathering dust.

Policy control is the chief control operant of any school board. When this responsibility is given up by the local school board, external forces tend to intervene in policy matters and local control is jeopardized. Policy has several specific characteristics. First and foremost, policy sets forth the purposes that the school programs are to achieve. They are related to a general area of major importance to the school system and citizenry. A policy is a broad statement that allows for freedom of interpretation and execution. It is equivalent to legislation and commonly is applicable over long periods of time. Policies are the primary responsibility of the school board and can only be adopted by the school board. A policy serves to answer the question, "What to do?"

When local school board control is weakened, external forces tend to enter into the business of the school. Local school-community purposes of education give way to external mandates and curricular program requirements that must be implemented if certain external funds are to be appropriated. Of primary importance is the probable loss of internal school-community interest and support. Student interests and needs are determined by external forces as opposed to school-community members with the leadership of an informed and qualified school board membership.

4. The Issue of Poor Student Academic Achievement in Schools Today

Criticism of public education programs and practices has been an ongoing practice in educational history. For example, sixty years ago, James Conant Bryant published his best-selling book *The American High School Today* which had a major influence on educational reforms at the time. Among his reform statements were his recommendations to consolidate high schools into larger bodies for the purpose of extending curricular offerings, changing of teacher certification whereby independent bodies could no longer certify teachers, and he recommended the controversial practice of de facto segregation of students that segregated students in fact but not according to the requirements of law. Perhaps no other educational statement since has had the effect on education reform that Conant's book had in 1959. Yet, we still hear reform statements that include Conant's recommendations as set forth above.

5. The Issue of the Inability to Attract and Retain Quality Administrative and Teacher Personnel

All teachers in America's public school classrooms are fully trained to lead a classroom, or are they? The answer is that they are not. Cano (2018b, August 23) reported that nearly 7,200 teaching certificates have been issued to teachers in Arizona who aren't fully trained for teaching. In fact, since 2015, the number of Arizona teaching certificates issued to teachers who aren't fully trained has increased by more than 400 percent according to the state's Department of Education data as analyzed by Cano and the *Arizona Republic* newspaper personnel. The issuance of teaching certificates to teachers not fully trained for the position has continued to increase each year since 2015. With this record, what would be expected regarding student performance on standardized tests and general education results?

The problem of attracting quality personnel into the teaching profession has been a problem historically. The problem of retaining their services is a related serious problem. The fact that teacher turnover commonly reaches 30 percent after the first year of teaching is generally well known and accepted. After five years, teacher loss reaches 50 percent. That is, of the group of teachers that enter teaching for the first time, after five years, 50 percent of this group has left the profession. We contend that both the recruitment of qualified teaching personnel and their retention are major problems; no organization can maintain stability with such high statistics of employee turnover.

Major changes in the way that professional teachers are recruited, assigned, developed, and compensated must be changed in order for the stability problem to be reversed. A later chapter of this book deals with these needed major program and personnel changes. If not implemented, education most likely will continue to be viewed as failing. Educators themselves are overly conservative when it comes to "promoting" the early interests of children and youth in the professional field of education. School field trips, classroom helpers, student clubs, and other in-school activities might turn the attention of talented students toward a personal interest in teaching as a sought-after career.

6. The Inhibiting Factor of Flawed Organizational Procedures and Mismanagement within the School District

The following example, set forth on page 1 of the *Arizona Republic* on June 26, 2018, served to underscore a major problem of public school failure. In the article, "State Will Take Over Murphy School District," the Arizona State Board of Education voted to appoint a receiver to oversee the district's operation among a $2.2 million spending deficit that publicly unraveled years of tension within the community and mismanagement in the district. It is beyond the scope of chapter 1 to discuss all of the issues and problems that surrounded the apparent "death" of this school district, but a number of problems related to financial woes, including disillusionment with district leadership, teacher/staff protests, angry parents, large classroom sizes, administrative resignations, loss of quality personnel, unfilled administrative positions, loss of school board members, and a variety of other dysfunctional operations within the school district were identified. But this is only one school district. Such difficulties are facing other school districts nationally as well.

ORGANIZATIONAL DEVELOPMENT AND SCHOOL IMPROVEMENT

During the gathering of ideas for this book, we visited schools and asked opinions of the personnel relative to school effectiveness. All too often we heard comments such as, "I've been an administrator in this school system for fifteen years and never been asked to serve on any system-wide committee or participated in the development of any major school policy" and "The school system is disengaged in that the central district office really does not know what we face at the local school level and we don't really know what the central staff is doing or thinking." Such statements make it clear that these school systems lack the qualities necessary for an effective learning culture to operate. We discuss the concept of organizational development (OD) in later chapters but note its purposes and importance in the following statement by Norton (2018):

> When effectively implemented, OD fosters a school climate that promotes student achievement, increases positive collaboration among members of the school/school system, gains the commitment of personnel toward viewing change as an ongoing phenomena that requires planned strategies that lead to problem solutions, promotes creative thinking and the development of new knowledge and skills that enhance worker self-fulfillment, fosters an open climate that facilitates effective communication and resolutions of inevitable conflicts, and operates on the premise that schools are people and that the human factor looms important in the achievement of program goals. (p. 11)

Organizational development (OD) has been defined in a variety of different ways but commonly is viewed as "an effort to improve the effectiveness of all components of an organization using the knowledge of behavior science" (Gupta, 2008, p. 1). OD encompasses four characteristics that serve to foster positive change: (1) Input: Preliminary planning. Diagnosing current production/achievement status, gathering from all sources within the organization, collecting and analyzing data of current results, preliminary procedures of action planning, implementing activities that serve toward *unfreezing behaviors* and procedures presently in place; (2) Transformation: Actions that center on new learning within the organization, steps that serve to gain the new knowledge and skills needed to achieve the changes needed within the organization. New learning serves to foster the confidence and motivators for personnel engagement in the action plans; (3) Output: The realization of changes in worker behavior, evaluation and assessment of change, results through the use of purposeful data gathering. Both production and human behavior changes are evaluated and assessed. Successful results are put into place by *re-freezing behaviors and procedures in place;* and (4) Feedback: The OD change model is not a one-time activity. Following each successful output change, a new cycle of change renewal is implemented (Norton, 2018, pp. 5–6).

THE MAJOR SUCCESS FACTORS OF PUBLIC EDUCATION: THE OTHER SIDE OF THE STORY

The *success factors* that are most commonly set forth in support of public education are: (1) the academic opportunities being provided by public education and its role of being a place where children can receive care, sustenance, safety, and the opportunity to learn; (2) education's availability/inclusiveness to all students including those with special needs; (3) the improvement of teacher preparation programs within institutions of higher education over the years; (4) the relative high percentage of high school graduates that enroll in college; and (5) the fact that education has produced a high level of social mobility and helped to create a shared culture that is essential to the maintenance of a democratic society (Kowal & Thomas, 2002).

Success Entry #1: The Success Factor of Learning Opportunities in the Nation's Public Schools

Successful public schools are ones that have gained the confidence of the school-community by creating an environment for teaching and learning and the school principal and faculty have answered the key questions of: Why does our school exist? What is our primary purpose? and What is our reason for being here? When each question is purposely explored, the answers fall on the concept that the school is for the provision of learning opportunities for all students inclusively; school leaders and staff are student advocates and as such center on opportunities that best reflect the individual interests and needs of each student. Learning opportunities are provided at the success level of each student. Student success widens the opportunity path for each individual.

By opportunities, we refer to the many opportunities that a public school education provides for growth and development. Such involvement provides the student more chances to do something different and better. As Eleanor Roosevelt said, "If you prepare yourself you will be able to grasp opportunity for broader experience when it appears." Opportunities to grow and develop occur in the academic arena, but also are provided in a social context. Students are interacting with other students, teachers, and adults, participating in athletics, clubs, and community events. Academic opportunities are provided in so many different professional, business, vocational, science, and civic areas not dismissing the areas of the fine arts. In later chapters, we contend that the opportunities for student participation in the profession of education should be promoted as well.

Success Entry #2: Education's Inclusiveness for All Students, Including Those with Special Needs

Inclusiveness represents one of the primary success factors of public education. Inclusiveness, whereby all students including those with disabilities are included in general-education facilities, was advanced by Madeleine Will, the former assistant secretary of education, in the late 1980s and early 1990s. The movement expanded into the belief that education should be ready to accept all students and a program be developed that meets the individual interests and needs of each individual. This concept differs from the concept of setting certain standards for each and every student to achieve; rather learning was based on what is termed the success level for each student.

In addition, inclusion in public school education is founded on a commitment to several basic principles: (1) every student is viewed as important for having the capacity to help achieve the purposes that the school has set forth; (2) every student is shown value and respect; (3) the school has developed an environment where students grow and develop in a learning culture; and (4) every child is accepted and has a personal sense of belonging.

Federal legislation has been passed to assure that a student is placed in the least restricted environment for learning. Such a provision does not give the parents or students the authority to determine what is best for the student's placement; as long as the classroom in which the student is placed allows for personal improvement, the courts have ruled that such placement meets the requirements of the law. The concept certainly represents one of the success factors of public education. Inclusiveness is discussed additionally in later chapters of the book.

Success Entry #3: The Improvement of Teacher Education Programs throughout Institutions of Higher Education over the Years

Teacher training has advanced from the institution of *teacher institutes* operated by county superintendents in the nineteenth century. Graduation from high school and attendance at a summer teacher institute commonly satisfied the preparation requirements for elementary school teachers. Over the years, normal schools that centered on two years of preparation for teachers gave way to four-year, college training in departments of education. Even though teachers in most every state are now required to have a four-year degree in education with state licensure in teaching, the demand for classroom teachers has introduced other ways and means for being allowed to serve in the classroom.

In addition, most every state has accompanying requirements for practicing teachers to earn college credits in appropriate subject-matter courses for renewal of the teacher's license. A common practice today, however, is for a teacher to gain credits by pursing a master's degree. Such a step not only tends to satisfy license requirements but also results in moving upward on the salary schedule. The major criticism of this practice, however, is that such a practice does not serve to improve the teacher's classroom performance in that, all too often, his or her work has been done in the area of administrative supervision.

Although education success entry #3 does focus on teacher preparation and improvement, both teacher and administrative preparation are being greatly criticized today. That is, although teacher preparation has improved greatly over the years, teacher performance is viewed as being unsatisfactory by many critics. This topic is discussed in-depth in a later chapter of the book.

Success Entry #4: The Relative High Number of High School Graduates Who Enter College

Statistics concerning the percentage of high school graduates who enter college have been relatively consistent in recent years, although reported statistics do differ. In the year 2013, 66.2 percent of high school graduates enrolled in college. Three years later in 2016, the statistic rose to 69.7 percent or 31.5 percent higher. We view that as a success statistic for public schools. After all, some graduates enroll in vocational education programs, join some branch of the military service, or enter some other positive career in the world of work.

We are well aware of the critical facts that college dropouts are high and that too many universities report that, according to the results of the respected ACT (American College Test), students come to them from the public schools unprepared for college. As reported by NBC News (Chuck, 2015), just over half of all college students actually graduate.

In spite of the less than positive information reported in the foregoing section, we retain the factor of high school graduates entering college as a success factor for public schools. The consideration of having two-thirds of the public school graduates enrolling in college, in our view, establishes the fact that the large majority of students have learned the value of education and have been motivated to try to fulfill this important objective As one interviewee said to us, "Even though I did not make it through college, I have learned the importance of supporting my kids in that pursuit." We discuss the topic of educating students about the education profession in later chapters of the book.

Success Education Factor #5: The fact that education has produced a high level of social mobility and helped to create a shared culture that is essential to the maintenance of a democratic society and enhances one's potential for success in adult life.

The importance of public education for the retention of a democratic society has been emphasized by our national presidents from the time of our first national president, George Washington, in 1779. As he commented in his welfare address to the nation, "The more homogeneous our Citizens can be made in these particulars, the greater will be our prospect of permanent union; and primary object of each a national institution should be the eduction of our youth in the science of *government*." Ulysses S. Grant stated that "The free school is the promoter of that intelligence which is to preserve us as a nation." As stated by Lyndon B. Johnson, "From the very beginning of our nation, we have felt a fierce commitment to the idea of education for everyone. It fixed itself into our democratic creed." and as stated by President Obama, "Our public education system is the key to opportunity for millions of children. . . . It needs to be the best in the world."

Give thought to the social relationships that students experience in grades K–12. Yes, bullying, disobedience, and other uncivil behaviors occur all too often in our schools. These negatives should serve as learning experiences for the parties involved. Social activities, cooperative relationships, leadership opportunities, along with both winnings and losses, are most often experienced in the public school environment. Lessons of courtesy, for example, are common in a school environment that are not always available in the home.

We were told the story of one teacher who taught senior class members how to introduce themselves or a friend to their parents or to some other person of renown. A seemingly unimportant courtesy, but one of needed civility. Is it "Mother, I would like you to meet my friend, Janice" or is it

"Janice, I would like you to meet my mother?" Or is it, "Grandmother, this is my friend, Janice" or "Janice, this is my mom and dad." Propriety calls for presenting the younger person to the older or more esteemed person: "Senator Smith, this is my mother and father."

The foregoing discussion is a bit pretentious, perhaps, but social ability is high on the list of social maturity. Can you identify other public school programs and activities that served to promote your social demeanor? High ability in math, science, and reading commonly receives the credit for being what's important in school learning. Student tests on social and civil values are seldom or never administered. The lack of student discipline is a common complaint of schools today. We contend that the improvement of student social skills and civil behaviors should indeed be one of the public school's important purposes. A school as a learning organization makes lessons learned–whether good or bad–available to all staff.

NEVERTHELESS, THE CRITICISM OF PUBLIC EDUCATION REMAINS WITH US

Criticism relative to public education in America and lack of high-quality scholarship on the part of students are high on the list of criticism on the part of the citizenry. Determining valid and reliable data on the academic standing of students in the United States is difficult at best. Not that academic achievement of public school students is not widely reported, but the reliability and validity of the data, the selection and makeup of the students who were included in the achievement testing, how the tests were administered and what student population(s) were included in the testing outcomes are not always clear. For example, is the makeup of eighth-grade students in the United States the same as eighth-grade students in all other countries?

In every research report that we examined for any particular student achievement results, some follow-up criticism of the research report or the organization that conducted the study commonly was brought forth by some other "authority" that commented on the "flaws" in the research methodology or the bias of the group that administered the study.

To illustrate further the point of research pronouncements and following criticism of the conclusions reached, we present the work of Berliner and Biddle (1995) titled, *The Manufactured Crisis*. The authors contended that the attack on American schools in the early 1980s was largely an unwarranted and manufactured plot of right-wing school voucher advocates. A strong support of American education is supported. In a following review of the Berliner and Biddle manufactured crisis book, Lawrence C. Stedman (1995) strongly criticized Berliner and Biddle's book by stating that he was sympathetic to the authors' concerns, but as a scholar himself, who specializes in this kind of material, found the analysis of Berliner and Biddle deeply flawed and misleading. He commented that the analysis mischaracterized the test score decline data, mishandled the international findings, and failed to acknowledge students' continuing low levels of academic achievement.

Nevertheless, it appears that the low levels of student achievement commonly reported in the literature are sealed in the minds of American citizens and a variety of reasons is set forth by the citizenry as to why this underachievement of American students is occurring. In chapter 3, we detail recommendations for meeting the challenge of low student achievement.

At the outset, the misconception that every eighth-grade student is to meet the same standard of achievement academically is flawed. It is similar to setting the height of 3½ feet for all eighth-grade students to clear in the high jump by the end of the year. One group of students will clear the heights on their first try. A second group would likely clear that height by the end of grade eight. A certain group of eighth-graders will not be able to clear 3½ feet at the end of the school year. Few persons would disagree with the fact that students differ, but education programs commonly require every student to meet the same levels of academic performance.

POST-CHAPTER QUIZ

Take just a few minutes to complete the following chapter quiz. The following ten multiple-choice questions serve as a review of important information that sets the stage for the following chapters.

Directions: Circle the best answer to each question that follows. Then check your response with the correct answers set forth at the end of the quiz.

1. One primary contention set forth in chapter 1 is that historically there has been:

    a. little or no criticism of public school education across the fifty states.
    b. little or no support of public school education across the fifty states.
    c. much criticism of public school education, but all such criticism has been proven unfounded by specific research findings.
    d. a specific equal and opposite response made to virtually every criticism directed toward public school education.

e. sufficient available research on the quality of public school education to state that it is not failing in any sense of the word.

2. Which of the following factors are *not* viewed as an inhibitor to the success of public education in America?

    a. inadequate financial support
    b. inequities in program opportunities among the states
    c. widening loss of local control of public education
    d. the percentage of high school graduates that continue their education by entering college
    e. unsatisfactory student academic performance

3. Statistics relative to the financial support of public education have revealed that the ability to pay for public school education:

    a. is virtually equal among the fifty states.
    b. differs as much as 6 to 1 with the richest state's property value being six times that of the poorest state.
    c. differs only at the rate of 2 to 1.
    d. is based on the amount of product sales since public school monies depend on this tax source.
    e. is determined by the state government differentials between sales income and purchasing costs.

4. Criticism of public school education has been:

    a. an ongoing practice in educational history.
    b. a matter of poor school board policy decisions.
    c. a political difference between the republican and democratic parties.
    d. due to the federal teachers' association attempts to control teachers' salaries.
    e. on an increase of 5 percent annually since the passing of the teacher tenure law in the 1940s.

5. Historically, public school education has been viewed as:

    a. a federal responsibility.
    b. a state function.
    c. a local responsibility.
    d. a federal concern, a state responsibility, and a local function.

6. Which entry below commonly is considered to be the *primary* responsibility of a local school board?

    a. the hiring of the teaching staff
    b. public relations
    c. the hiring of the school superintendent
    d. school district governance policy development
    e. professional negotiations with the school district's personnel
    f. none of the above

7. The five U.S. states that were ranked highest in educational quality in one major research report were:

    a. among those states with the lowest per-pupil support funding.
    b. among those states with the highest per-pupil support funding.
    c. considered to be in the medium of per-pupil support funding.
    d. states that did not include athletics or elementary school recess in their local school programs.
    e. states that had a special education tax on all goods sold within the state.

8. Virtually every report or study that centers on the quality of public education in America underscores the importance of:

    a. establishing a mandatory system of student achievement accompanied by an in-grade retention system that demands the achievement of established grade standards for every subject and grade level in the school system.
    b. a change of school organization from the traditional K–12 school organization to an open-classroom system whereby the students themselves choose what they need to learn that day or that term in an open classroom setting.
    c. federal support and control of public school curriculum offerings and the instructional methods to accompany them.
    d. using ability level separation of students especially in the subject areas of reading, math, and science.
    e. all of the above.
    f. none of the above.

9. When all is said and done, it is clear that public education in America:

   a. is failing.
   b. is a success.
   c. has identifiable factors that inhibit high-quality education for all students everywhere.
   d. has identifiable factors that promote quality education for all students everywhere.
   e. none of the above.
   f. all of the above.

10. The contents in chapter 1 tend to suggest that:

    a. public school education in the United States indeed is failing.
    b. public school education in the United States indeed is succeeding.
    c. public education in the United States can be "saved" if only local school districts would give priority to professional development programs for all professional staff.
    d. traditional public education in the United States would be privatized and become competitive among the various "business parties" similar to competitive parties in business and industry.
    e. none of the above.
    f. all of the above.

POST-QUIZ, TRUE OR FALSE

1. Research studies and collected evidence make it clear that public school education is failing. True____ or False____
2. Among the many critical factors facing public school education, the factor of financial support is seldom named among the top ten problems and issues. True____ or False____
3. Those individuals in education with some experience commonly name the lack of research as a cause of educational failure. True____ or False____
4. Unfortunately, no one has ever set forth a recommendation for changes in compensating school personnel that would theoretically improve the hiring and retention of teachers. True____ or False____

5. Research evidence has made it clear that education inequities among the states can be remedied by the federal government's intervention into public school education. True____ or False____
6. The statistics relative to the fifty states have shown that the ability to support education financially differs on a ratio of 6 to 1. True____ or False____
7. Successful school programs set forth academic standards that every child must meet before moving ahead. True____ or False____
8. Basic research accomplished in education is one factor that underscores the current success of public school operations. True____ or False____
9. Interestingly enough, no authority or educational group has ever set forth specific alternatives for compensating teachers in public schools. True____ or False____
10. Public education in America is viewed as a state responsibility. True____ or False____

DISCUSSION OF THE POST-CHAPTER QUIZ

We introduce a post-chapter quiz in chapter 1 to underscore its purpose of examining the wide division of views relative to the current effectiveness of public education in America and examining the major reasons why educational reforms seldom result in long-term improvements or wide public acceptance of implemented reform interventions.

Quiz question #1. In question #1, the reader was asked to complete the question: One primary contention is that historically there has been which one of the five possible responses? The best response to the question is "d," "a specific equal and opposite response made to virtually every criticism directed toward public school education." There are multiple examples of this troublesome controversy. For example, McSpadden's article "Public Schools Aren't Failing" (2015) was countered by DeSilver's article (2017) "U.S. Students' Academic Achievement Still Lags That of Their Peers in Many Other Countries."

The question for our consideration centers on what professional leadership and program promotions are to be pursued in depth. Even the matter of educational support for public education has its pro and con audiences. In many instances, the yes or no answer is vested in an educational matter that is definitely political in nature. The promotion of charter schools, local school control, school curricular offerings, and school funding are prime examples of political education decision matters.

Quiz Question #2. The correct response to question #2 is "d," "the percentage of high school graduates that continue their education by entering college." In the year 2009, an all-time high of 70.1 percent of the high school graduates were enrolled in college. In a later 2013 report, this percentage had dropped to 65.9 percent but raised again to 69.7 percent in 2016. In the more recent years between 2011 and 2016, the percentage of enrolled high school graduates increased only 1.4 percent. The highest enrollment of recent high school graduates was in 2009, with an enrollment figure of 70.1 percent. The high school graduation figure has tended to retain its relative high percentage of college enrollees in spite of increases in high school student dropout rates, governmental emphasis on vocational/technical education in the 1960s, and the calls for military service on the part of male and female graduates during the various military "conflicts" over the years.

Some persons would argue that college entrance data on the part of high school graduates are an inhibiting factor as opposed to a success factor of public education. Many other factors serve to influence such decisions, including job opportunities, ability to pay higher college tuition fees, academic standing, and vocational/technical program interests.

Quiz Question #3. The answer to question #3 is "b," whereby the richest states' ability to pay is six times that of other poorest states. Since local taxes on property values serve specifically for education support, the inequities of funding are major concerns for giving each child in the United States a fair and equal opportunity for a quality education. Various state financial support methods have been designed by the several states. Nevertheless, major differences in property values make equalizing financial support per child a difficult situation. Providing a required minimum education support might well be relatively easy to do for some school districts but may also place a hardship on districts with limited property values. This issue is discussed additionally in a later chapter.

Quiz Question #4. Criticism of public school education has been "an ongoing practice," entry "a," historically. Who should be educated? How should education be financially supported? What should be emphasized in the public school curriculum? Should student retention in-grade be discontinued or increased? Should standardized testing of student academic performance be increased and used as a basis for determining a teacher's salary? Should recess at the elementary school level be discontinued? Who or what body should be solely responsible for determining the curricular program of a public school? Why does the state have so many separate school districts that need separate school boards, more principals, and more school facilities? Does class size really make a difference in student achievement? What specific program interventions would actually serve to end the criticism of education in the United States? Will such a solution ever be found?

Quiz Question #5. Historically, public school education has been viewed as "d," a federal concern, state responsibility, and a local function. It has been noted that the U.S. Constitution makes no mention of education, but the

Tenth Amendment leaves those matters not specifically mentioned in the document to the states and its people. Thus, such matters as vocational/ technical education, physical education, students with special needs, improved math/science instruction, and many others have been high on the list of federal concerns. Educational interventions by the federal government, state government, and other parties have lessened the local control of education. The development of policy manuals for local school districts by the National Association of School Boards is a prime example. Retaining local control of education, state mandates, and federal interventions have been major debates on educational matters historically.

Quiz Question #6. Which entry below commonly is considered to be the *primary* responsibility of the local school board? The answer is "f," none of the above. We do understand that many knowledgeable individuals would have circled entry "c," the hiring of the school superintendent, or perhaps entry "b," public relations. However, as stated by Norton (2017). "The development of school district policies is the most important responsibility of school boards nationally. . . . Effective policy development is the crux of successful school operation" (p. vii). Administrative procedures, local school control, professional development program activities, and operational success are inextricably tied to the effective policies that focus on the goals and objectives which the school district is destined to achieve.

Quiz Question #7. The five states that were ranked highest in education quality in one major research report were among those states with the highest per-pupil support funding, answer "b." For example, in one study of education quality, the state of Massachusetts was ranked #1. That state was also among those states with the highest per-pupil financial support. Although this relationship does not ring perfect for all states, the fact that per-pupil spending is related to education quality is notable in reliable study reports.

Quiz Question #8. Virtually, every report or study that centers on the quality of education in America underscores the importance of: "f," none of the above. Although each of the five entries set forth as possible answers has been proposed in some form by some body over time, no research report or *long-term* school program has featured any of these five outcomes (e.g., mandatory system of student achievement accompanied by an in-grade retention system; change from K–12 school organization to an open classroom system; federal support and control of education; separation of students by ability level). We do emphasize long-term programs since similar organizational arrangements have been implemented for brief time periods historically.

Quiz Question #9. When all is said and done, it is clear that public school education in America "has identifiable factors that inhibit quality education for students everywhere" (answer "c") and "promotes quality education for students everywhere" (answer "d"). Both "c" and "d" responses appear to be in order. The question is vested in what approach is to be taken for reaching the objective of making education in America the best of all worlds. Is it best to give primary attention to improving and/or reimagining the factors that are inhibiting quality education or is it best to focus on those factors and are fostering quality education in public education? The oversimplification of an answer to these questions is to focus on both. The following chapters of the book center on both approaches. However, reimagining education rather than additional attention to more reforms is given emphasis in future chapters.

Quiz Question #10: The contents of chapter 1 tend to suggest that "e," none of the above responses is completely correct. That is, no conclusions can be reached to set forth the result that public education is indeed failing or succeeding. Characteristics of failure were identified and the same thing can be said for education's success. Our approach to this result is that researched innovations must be taken to keep improving and extending those factors that are having successful educational results and revolutionary concepts must be implemented to extinguish those factors that are failing and establish revolutionary changes in educational practice.

ANSWERS TO THE TRUE OR FALSE POST-QUIZ

True and false question #1 is False, #2 is False, #3 is False, #4 is False, #5 is False, #6 is True, #7 is False, #8 is False, #9 is False, and #10 is True. Various studies have set forth a variety of reasons why public schools are failing. Thus, statement #1 is false. The fact is that there is a wide difference of opinion as to whether public schools are failing or doing well. In regard to statement #2, financial support for education raises near or at the top of reasons why public schools are failing. Chapter 3 makes it clear that statement #3 is false. Research is seldom mentioned within education discussions for supporting or criticizing public school outcomes. Chapter 3 discusses various needed changes in public school programming, and changes in the way teachers are compensated is one of them. Thus statement #4 is false. No such research has been set forth regarding the intervention of the federal government for "saving" public schools in America; statement #5 is false. Statement #6 is true; the ability to support education differs considerably among the fifty states. The ratio of 6 to 1 represents the extent to which financial support for education differs from highest to lowest ability. Statement #7 is false. Students differ and thus one set standard sets forth an inequitable expectation for student achievement results. There has been no such research on educational standards as suggested in statement #8; thus #8 is false. It is true that . . . and others have recommended major changes in the way public school teachers are compensated. Thus, statement #9 is false. Question #10 is true. Historically, public education has been viewed as a federal concern, a state responsibility, and a local function. However, the increasing involvement of state and federal agencies into local public school affairs has influenced these responsibilities considerably. In short, local school functions have been mandated increasingly by state and federal agencies.

THOUGHTS ON WHAT IS RIGHT WITH PUBLIC EDUCATION

A general statement by Kowal and Thomas (2002) serves to sum up what commonly is viewed by the citizenry as to what is right with public education:

> American tradition of public education began with Jefferson's ideal of an aristocracy based on talent and not on inherited wealth and privilege. Ever since its inception, the grand tradition of public education has undergone significant changes. It has been a crucial part of the immigrant experience, allowing the children of first-generation Americans to achieve a level of success that would not have been possible in their native countries. Indeed, education has produced a level of social mobility that is unmatched in most countries. It is public education that helps create a shared culture that is essential in any democracy. Public education also nurtures the financial health of any society.

KEY CHAPTER IDEAS AND RECOMMENDATIONS

- Reports and opinions regarding the quality of public schools differ widely. When one criticism of education is set forth that education is failing, another opinion comes forth claiming that public school education is better than ever before. The major criticisms of public school education center on the lack of financial support, inequities in the quality of education programs within the states and school districts, the extension of state and federal agencies into the control of local education programs, the incompetency of both teacher and administrative personnel, and poor student academic achievement.
- Empirical evidence makes it quite clear that American citizenry not only differs on whether the public schools are failing or not, but they differ widely on the purposes of public school education. One most frequently stated purpose is that of the need for an educated citizenry sustaining a democratic form of government. Others tend to be of the opinion that public school education should focus on resolving the many social issues being encountered in the nation that tend to find their way into the public schools of America as well. It is clear that both of these purposes need to be reimagined and resolved.

- The highest ranking of states relative to quality education is closely correlated with the highest per pupil spending; that is the highest-ranking states for quality also spend most on per-pupils education support.
- The ability to pay for education among the states differs from 6 to 1. That is, the state with the highest property value has six times the property value of the lowest state's property value.
- The lack of policy development on the part of local school boards has resulted in a lessening of their local control of the education program. The responsibility for developing policy at the local school level has been turned over to state school board associations in an increasing number of cases. It is recommended that this practice be stopped. The primary responsibility of school boards should be the development of guiding school policy. School board associations have many other things to do. Just assisting local school districts in establishing an effective codification system for policy manuals is one such service.
- The increasing inability of school districts to recruit and retain high-quality teacher and administrative personnel is among education's leading problems. Quality instruction and high-level student learning will never take place without the presence of high-quality education personnel.
- Administrative mismanagement within public schools looms as a major inhibitor of quality education. Mismanagement has major implications for education financial support, professional education preparation programs, and competency performance on the job.
- The lack of major research units within the local school districts and state education offices looms as a primary cause of public school failure. The failure to establish high-quality research programs within local school districts and state departments of eduction is a critical error on the part of educational services within the fifty states. In professions such as medicine and other successful business and industrial practices, research is the foundation of progress and success. If a cure for cancer or Alzheimer's disease was found in medical research, practicing professionals around the world would have the results of the research in place as a first priority. In education, when viable results of research are found in relation to student retention, class size, student learning styles, and other practices, educators tend to continue doing what they have been doing for many years.
- The hiring of teacher personnel who have not completed a training program is more serious perhaps than is realized by the general public. No one would knowingly go to a physician, lawyer, or other professional service provider who had not completed satisfactorily the preparation requirements for licensing. Yet, this practice in education has been increasing and certain testing results are reflecting its outcome.
- Major success factors in public school education include the wide range of academic opportunities that students have available for learning, the inclu-

siveness of public schools and openness for children of all abilities and interests, the improvement of teacher preparation programs over the years, the high percentage of high school graduates that enroll in college, the program guidance given to students relative to the culture of the American society, the importance of education for maintaining a democratic form of national governance, and supporting the American concept of a free enterprise system can be credited in large part to the work of America's public education provisions.

Yet, criticism of America's public school system remains. The following chapters of the book center on what it will take to reimagine education in our country. Educational reform is not the term that we have in mind. Rather, revolutionary reimagining of ways for making public education the best of all worlds will serve the discussions provided in the chapters that follow.

DISCUSSION QUESTIONS

1. Assume that you are a member of a debate team that is debating the following resolution: Resolved: Public-Education is Failing. Take sides as a member of the "pro" or the "con" debate team and write out your two-minute opening statement for your team.
2. Put on your reimagination hat and give thought to the preparation of teachers as you understand it today. If you are or have been a teacher, what changes would you recommend in the preparation program in which you engaged? If not a teacher, rely on what you know and have observed relative to teaching performance. How might you add to or change the preparation programs for teachers or what provisions in teacher preparation do you believe most significant? Can you come up with a revolutionary preparation program model?
3. Chapter 1 set forth the statement that the quality of an education system cannot exceed the quality of teachers. What does this concept suggest for needed changes in public education practices and financial support?
4. Take a moment to review the success factors for education set forth in chapter 1. What additional success factor(s) might you add to that listing? Set forth a brief defense of your response.
5. At a parent-teacher meeting at your school, the matter of increasing student fees for certain subjects, sport's participation, and related program activities came to the floor. One parent commented that she believed that the American way was that each student was assured the right to a free and equal education. What might be your response to the parent's belief?

CASE STUDY

Just a Matter of Working Harder or Is it?

Principal Woolhether was meeting with the school faculty to give them the unfortunate news that their school had just received a rating of "C" as being underperforming.

"We need to act and act now," said Principal Woolhether. "I am required to respond to this situation within two months with details of what we plan to do to reverse this failing trend. Of course, the test results focus on math, science, and reading scores, so this has to be our major focus."

"What changes are to be made in our program activities and instructional strategies?" asked Mr. Evans. "What about the instructional resources that we need and the student apathy that all of us are facing? What about the new textbooks that have been on order for at least two years?"

"I am concerned about the present mandate that sets forth the instructional methods for the teaching of reading," inserted Miss Ortez. "It's like someone is looking over my shoulder and telling me how to teach. I took two courses on reading for my bachelor's degree and believe that I know something about the subject of reading."

"Yeah," responded Coach Adams, who also taught science. "Do we get new kids?"

After the laughter died down, Principal Woolhether cautioned the faculty about making excuses and went on to say, "We need to change and the sooner the better. Just setting forth excuses will not suffice. Now, let's all get to work!"

Case Study Follow-Up Exercise

1. What seems to be missing from Principal Woolhether's closing remarks of "Now, let's get back to work!"?
2. How might the information on organizational development (OD) set forth in the chapter be most helpful in the study case? Although the case calls for a response on the matter within two months, what information might be sent back as a first response in order for an effective OD procedure to be planned, implemented, evaluated, and assessed?

REFERENCES

Barber, M., & Mourshed, M. (2007, September). *How the world's best performing schools come out on top*. New York: McKinsey & Company. From the web: http://mckinseysociety.com/how-the-worlds-best-performing-schools-come-out-on-top

Berliner, D. C., & Biddle, B. J. (1996). *The manufactured crisis: Myths, fraud, and the attack on America's public schools*. New York: Basic Books, an Imprint of Perseus Books Group.

Bernardo, R. (2017). *The quality of public education in the United States.* Washington, DC: WalletHub, Evfolution Finance, Inc.

Cano, R. (2018a, June 26). State will take over Murphy school district. *Arizona Republic*, p. 1A. Phoenix, AZ.

Cano, R. (2018b, August 23). Thousands of teachers lack complete formal training. *Arizona Republic*, p. 1A. Phoenix, AZ.

Chen, G. (2017, July 12). Public school v. private school. *The Washington Post.* Washington, DC.

Chuck. E. (2015, November 18). *Just over half of all college students actually graduate, report finds.* NBC News.

DeSilver, D. (2017, February 15). U.S students' academic achievement still lags that of their peers in many other countries. *Pew Research Center.* From the web: http://www.pewresearch.org/author/ddesilver/

Fedewa, L. J. (2014). American schools are failing. *The Washington Times.* Washington, DC.

Gates, B., & Gates, M. (2017). *What we do.* From the web: http://k12educationl.gatesfoudation.org/

Gupta, A. (2008). What is organizational development? *Practical Management.* Practical Management Institute. Phoenix, AZ: author.

Jaeger, K. (2015, July 13). This map is a powerful illustration of the wealth gap in the U.S. *attn:.* From the web: https://archive.attn.com/stories/2347/united-states-disproportionate-income-inequality

Klein, J. (2011, June). The failure of American schools. *The Atlantic.* Boston, MA.

Kowal J., & Thomas, T. M. (2002). What's right with public education: Fastback. *ERIC.* ERIC Number: EAD478534.

McSpadden, K. (2015). Public schools aren't failing. Special to the observer. *Viewpoint.*

Norton, M. S. (2017). *A guide for educational policy governance: Effective leadership for policy development.* Lanham, MD: Rowman & Littlefield Publishers.

Norton, M. S. (2018). *Dealing with change: The effects of organizational development on contemporary practices.* Lanham, MD: Rowman & Littlefield Publishers.

Norton, M. S., Kelly, L. K., & Battle, A. R. (2012). *The principal as student advocate: A Guide for doing what's best for all students.* Larchmont, NY: Eye On Education.

Rampell, C. (2014). Actually, public education is getting better, not worse. *The Washington Post.* Washington, DC.

Room 241 Team (2018). *Public education costs per pupil by state rankings.* A blog by Concordia University at Portland, Oregon.

Sager, J. (2013). *Education system in America is failing: Why American public schools are failing.* From the web: Theprogressivecynic.com

Schneider, J. (2016). America's not-so-broken education system: Do U.S. schools really need to be disrupted? *The Atlantic.*

Stedman, L. G. (1996, January 4). *Review of Berliner & Biddle, The Manufactured Crisis.* Research Gate. Mary Lou Fulton Teachers College, Arizona State University, Tempe. From the web: https://www.researchgate.net/publication/49609879_Review_of_Berliner_Biddle_The_Manufactured_Crisis

Chapter Two

Education Futurology Based on Current Trends and Conditions

PRIMARY CHAPTER GOAL

The need to improve today's educational programs for students is emphasized in relation to their implications for preparing them for successful living in the years ahead.

YOUR GUESS IS AS GOOD AS MINE

Futurology is defined as a study of future possibilities based on current trends and conditions of a thing that might happen. For engagement purposes, take a few minutes to respond to the following "future" quiz. In each case, you are asked to check your opinion as to whether or not the prediction will be in place by 2030, approximately ten years from now. Respond to each of the predictions for the year 2030 and then check your responses with the answers that follow.

1. By the year 2030, scientists will be using hand implants to restore the freedom of movement that the spinal cord takes away. Will be in place____ Will not be in place____
2. A deep learning AI search engine that sorts hours of footage with ease to quickly locate a specific person or vehicle across an entire state. Will be in place____ Will not be in place____
3. Long stays in hospitals will change. No longer will women have to stay in the hospital after giving birth for ten days or more. Instead, it

will be common for women to reduce the time by 2030 to a twenty-four-hour turnaround. Will be in place____ Will not be in place____
4. The workforce will be quite different by 2030. Work specialties, as we have known them for years, will change whereby diverse teams will work on specific problems as opposed to implementing specific specialties. Will be in place____ Will not be in place____
5. In 2030, permanent workers within a company will be reduced substantially. Nonpermanent employees will make up approximately 40 percent of the average company's total employees. Will be in place____ Will not be in place____

If you checked each response, will be in place by 2030, you will have been correct but perhaps a bit late. Contemporary reports have stated that each of the foregoing "changes" already are in contemporary practices. For example, Jodi Williams (2017, February 9) reported major changes that will take place in the years ahead. Multinational corporations are having their teams of employees collaborate at different offices across the planet. The point is that similar changes in educational programs and practices will be greatly influenced by both ongoing environmental and internal changes that will inevitably occur. In the following section, we discuss other future changes that will impact education in America's schools.

IS ORAL AND WRITTEN COMMUNICATION GOING AWAY?

It is well known that many school districts nationally no longer give instruction in cursive writing. Of course, communication today is by use of the smart phone, computer, or other technical resources. Yet, a study by the Partnership for 21st Century Skills reported that nearly 90 percent of employers viewed high school graduate entrants as being "deficient" in communication. Authorities have stressed the fact that effective oral and written communication is of paramount importance. Nichols (2015, November 5) listed effective oral and written communication as one of the seven skills that students will always need. She notes that despite advances in technology, these skills never lessen in their importance for the best communication.

CRITICAL THINKING AND STUDENTS' EFFECTIVENESS

Not only is the correct use of grammar and language use important today, but such skills are closely related to clear thinking and effective understanding of messaging and personal effectiveness that will be of prime importance in the years ahead. That is, critical thinking is underscored as being of great importance in virtually every report of knowledge and skill needed for success. A question of paramount importance is: Should schools be focusing on the teaching of specific skills for today's work positions or be focusing on critical thinking skills that are perceived as being needed for the jobs of tomorrow? In any case, many authorities place critical thinking as the most important skill that schools should be teaching. *Critical thinking* commonly is defined as the analysis of facts to form a judgment.

Critical thinking is founded on thought, assessment, and evaluation that go far beyond the memorizing and recalling of facts and figures. Rather it delves deeply into thought processes that include analyzing, evaluating, synthesizing, and assessing various solutions to the problem being encountered. The individual that is using critical thinking is using his or her skills to resolve problems. As stated by Llopis (2013), "Problem solving is the essence of what leaders exist to do" (p. 1). They are implementing creative thinking by implementing the skills of developing, examining, questioning, debating, devising, formulating, articulating, and identifying relative to the problem(s) that exist in contemporary times.

OLD WINE IN OLD BOTTLES

The well-known scientific problem-solving model is a first cousin of an effective thinking process. When the five-step problem-solving model is used by groups in a shared, collaborative, and systematic way, it serves several beneficial purposes. When effectively applied, the model not only serves toward the resolution of a problem being faced but most often results in program improvements. For this reason, the scientific model is reviewed in the following section.

The scientific problem-solving model commonly is defined as follows:

Step 1. *Defining the problem*

The specific problem at hand is evaluated and assessed in terms of several questions. Specifically, what is the nature of the problem? What are the troublesome symptoms surrounding the problem? Who is affected by the problem and are these groups/individuals involved in the plans to resolve it? Why wasn't the problem and its solution addressed much earlier? How urgent is the problem and how important is it that it be resolved? How might our advance planning have obviated the problem in the first place? Such consideration might serve as an improvement message for future program changes.

Step 2. *Analyzing the problem*

Once the troublesome symptoms of the problem are identified, the effort is placed on further analyzing the basic causes of the problem and how and whom it is affecting. Some authorities view step 2 as determining the "root causes" of the problem. Such information helps to determine the seriousness of the problem, who it is affecting, and helps to further define and clarify the matter. Are the causes of the problem within the jurisdiction of the local school or school system? This information gives further clarification of the problem causes and the nature of solutions that might be available.

Step 3. *Focusing on logical solutions to the matter*
In view of the problem as now defined, brainstorming various solutions serves a positive purpose. Although each "possible" solution is given consideration, those solutions that are viewed as having minimal impact on the problem at hand are eliminated and all solutions with good potential for resolution are examined once again. Which solution has the best possibility for implementation, has the most support among the persons who will be affected by the solution, is most cost-effective, is most manageable, and is viewed as most beneficial for the human and material characteristics of the organization?

Step 4. *Select a solution*
Select the favored solution and initiate its implementation. Determine the person(s) who are most prepared and situated to lead in the initial planning for implementing the favored solution. Teams of members serve in the planning process by setting forth needed procedures, establishing development programs as fits the case, and setting the chosen plan in place. What resources are needed? Is staff development to be planned and implemented? What are the target dates for putting the new plan in place?

Step 5. *Implementation and evaluation of the new plan*
A PERT chart that establishes the primary target dates for the new plan's implementation and administration is established. Ongoing oversight on the plan's success and needed alterations are imperative. What program activities are to be monitored and assessed? What data are to be collected and evaluated? What related information such as actual progress, job satisfaction, cost figures, improvements in productivity, and needed interventions are determined as recommended? The positive climate characteristics of collaboration and cooperation continue throughout the process.

Models, such as the one just described, tend to assume that the leader(s) and related participants involved in the matter are all rational and able to address the environment in an intelligent and appropriate manner. Systems do not always have the capacity to sense, monitor, and scan the significant aspects of their environment. When this is not the case, the intelligence of the system breaks down. Thus, learning to learn for the purpose of self-organization becomes necessary.

NEW WINE IN NEW BOTTLES

Llopis (2013, November 4) sheds new light on the issue of problem solving. He catches the reader's attention by noting that so many problems keep mounting up that leaders find themselves taking shortcuts in an attempt to temporarily alleviate the turmoil and resulting tension. In the end, the leader fails to resolve the problem at hand and gets caught in the never-ending cycle of confusion that results. The point that catches the reader's eye is that problem solving is exactly what school leaders are hired to do. The leader has this primary responsibility for problem solving in spite of the fact that the school is a social organization with people who complicate the problem with the inevitability of internal politicking, self-promotion, power plays, politics, and other out-of-hand inhibitors such as lack of funding, limited resources, and other circumstances that inhibit effective productive activity. Problem solving is not always an easy matter and that is why effective collaborative leadership looms important.

Llopis further contended that the best leaders are the best problem solvers. Educational life is, in fact, problem solving. He further contends that an effective leader never views a problem as a distraction, rather it is viewed as an opportunity for fostering further improvement and possibly new interventions that have never come to mind. Improvement is directly related to change; problem resolutions serve as an enabler for continuous improvement and program interventions that were not previously foreseen. In this respect, Llopis's thoughts are revolutionary.

We applaud Llopis's stated recommendations for problem strategy implementation. He speaks of the need to focus on strategy, gathering the right people, working collaboratively, setting forth a plan of action, avoiding guessing, and using problem solving as an enabler for growth and development. In the mind of Llopis, the leader should embrace problem solving and the many unseen treasures that it represents; a revolutionary way of thinking. The Economist Intelligence Unit limited (2015) conducted a business survey and asked the question: Which of the following would you say are the most critical skills for employees in your organization to possess today?

Problem solving led the list of fourteen possible choices with a 50 percent response. Problem solving was viewed as a universal need according to the authority participants. Team working, communication, critical thinking, creativity followed with responses of 35 percent to 21 percent. Team working received a response of 35 percent and leadership was surprisingly low with an 18 percent response by participants. It is logical to assume that problem solving will be a skill of paramount importance in the future as well.

CRITICAL THINKING AND DECISION-MAKING: TWO INTERTWINED ENTITIES

We have identified critical thinking as one of the basic decision-making and problem-solving techniques. While critical thinking involves the serious examining of assumptions about a problem, decision-making is related more to a specific action. In short, decision-making is a product of critical thinking. The two concepts are intertwined and we cannot have one without the other. Critical thinking is one of the basic decision-making and problem-solving techniques.

Chapter 2 places an emphasis on the importance of collaboration and group thinking as being of primary importance for effective contemporary and future educational programming. One might ask the question: Is group decision-making more effective than individual decision-making relating to problem resolution? Although the literature on the effectiveness of individual vs. group decision-making tends to focus on the answer, "that it all depends," one study by Bombeck in the 1980s definitely supported the positive group decision-making strategy. The question set forth in Bombeck's study was as follows: Can teams make better decisions than individuals?

That is, can team involvement improve the decisions of the group as individuals? Bombeck studied the decision-making results of individuals and teams using different instruments that included a decision-making game, critical thinking appraisals, and so forth. He then compared the results of teams vs. individuals. The findings were as follows:

1. None of the four statistical hypotheses were rejected by the testing. The hypotheses contended that group decisions were better than decisions made by one individual. A comparison of team and individual results supported the superiority of team efforts. Of the fifty-nine respondents, only seven had better individual scores than the team scores.
2. Only one team out of fifteen teams had a lower score than the average of the teams' individual scores.
3. The study results reaffirmed earlier findings of researchers who had given serious consideration to group decision-making. Bombeck's study further suggested that improvement in group decision-making ability can be taught.

In any case, decisions relative to educational problems are seldom resolved in incidental faculty meetings. That is, specific collaborative strategies have more potential for gaining the best thinking of both individuals and groups. For this reason, we discuss three strategies that have proven beneficial in gaining the best thinking of group members, involving the organization's members in the decision-making process, and gaining the commitment of members toward the implementation of the group's "final decision" on a matter of mutual importance. We keep in mind that internal program improvement is commensurate with program change. Effective change requires the unfreezing of previous practices.

GROUP DECISION-MAKING STRATEGIES

Systems thinking and other participative arrangements for determining group opinion and/or problem solving tend to be problematic; internal change does not come easily. Several effective strategies have been found to be beneficial in the implementation of group problem solving (Norton, 2018). Gaining faculty input relative to such school matters as school policies and regulations, program provisions, budget priorities, student activities, teacher load, and other significant matters have been found to be satisfactorily determined by the use of such group processes as the Nominal Group Technique (NGT), the Delphi Technique, and Brainstorming.

Once again, we keep in mind that our guiding purpose is to find effective strategies for improving contemporary educational practices. Organizational leaders make decisions on the kinds of problems that face them on a daily basis. In the following section, the focus is on those difficult problems that tend to inhibit program progress. Commonly, these kinds of problems are accompanied by both pros and cons of acceptance and rejection; ones that tend to hinder positive human relations, school improvement, and the development of a learning culture within the school. Given a few minutes for discussion on an important problem during the weekly after-school faculty meeting seldom provides a satisfactory answer. A more planned sophisticated strategy is required. The Nominal Group Technique can provide what is needed.

The Nominal Group Technique (NGT) certainly is not new. It has been found to be effective for gaining the involvement of faculty members in the problem-solving activities being encountered.

Steps of the NGT are set forth as follows:

Step 1—*The problem at hand is defined as clearly as possible.* An assessment of the matter is discussed and examined with the information now in hand.

Step 2—*Participating group members set forth their ideas on the matter*, including his/her recommendations or solutions, in writing. Each member must participate; contributions are not anonymous.

Step 3—*There is a round robin recording of members' ideas.* One idea from each member's list is placed on the chalkboard or flip chart. The recording is continued until each member's list has been recorded.

Step 4—*A presentation and clarification of members' ideas is conducted.* Each member clarifies his/her ideas without any criticism or discussion by other members.

Step 5—*There is a consolidation of the ideas presented.* That is, similar ideas are consolidated by the agreement of the members concerned. If consensus is not reached, the ideas remain as stated.

Step 6—*Further clarification is provided.* A second opportunity for members is provided for members to clarify their idea(s). Once again, no criticism is permitted.

Step 7—*There is a first attempt to determine a best solution.* At this time, group members identify the "best" solutions set forth. Commonly, a "yes" or "no" response is sought regarding whether or not to retain the idea for further consideration. For example, group members might be asked to rank in order the three most important or relevant items on the list. Items with the highest number of "votes" are considered in the final vote.

Step 8—*The final selection.* If only one recommendation is to be selected or more than one entry is appropriate, a rank ordering of the entries is conducted. Or, each member selects one first choice from the remaining entries. The entry with the highest number for first choice is considered as the final selection.

The Delphi Technique differs from the NGT in that it frequently is conducted from a distance. Participants do not necessarily know one another and are not introduced to one another all during the exercise. The Delphi Technique is carried out commonly as follows:

1. The matter at hand sets the stage for the first procedure whereby a statement of questions is sent to each Delphi participant. The number of participants varies; as many as twenty or more participants might be involved in the process. Commonly, a list of questions or possible options or priorities is sent to the participants.
2. Participants react to each question or provide a clear statement of their position on the matter at hand. In the case that specific options are included in the first message to participants, some rating procedure such as a Likert scale is included for the participants' responses.

3. The members' response lists are returned and the monitor of the process compiles the results. These results are also sent to members for a second round of judgments. It is common for participants to be able to insert their own personnel recommendations on the matter at this point and time. That is, participants have a chance to reconsider their former position(s) on the matter and explain why they have changed their opinion on the matter.
4. The responses on round 2 are further reviewed by the monitor and ranked in light of the new inputs. The hope is that the responses are moving toward a definite consensus. However, it is common to have a third round of assessments if some consensus is not obtained.
5. The one advantage of the Delphi method is that of anonymous member domination. Also, other human relations problems that sometimes are present in face-to-face activities are avoided. Member agreements about important goals and other program matters provide an important initial step for follow-up organizational planning and implementation. Not only do the initial participants benefit, but their personal learning from the exercise serves to benefit their own school or school district's program as well.

GAINING NEW IDEAS FROM BRAINSTORMING

Brainstorming, as a method of problem solving, is nothing new. Various approaches to brainstorming have been implemented in practice. However, Gatty (2019, February 6) most recently set forth seven steps for implementing this strategy for improving decisions and resolving problems in the organization. Gatty underscores three specific benefits of brainstorming: (1) Business decision-making is strengthened by considering divergent points of view. As simplistic as this benefit might seem, the pros and cons that commonly accompany most every program activity in education are accompanied with major controversy; (2) business decision-making is improved by encouraging critical thinking; and (3) brainstorming builds more cohesive teams. As Gatty notes, brainstorming is, by nature, a collaborative experience.

We cite Gatty's article (2019, February 6) for the common way in which brainstorming is conducted:

1. Establish a goal: Identify the problem that will be solved from the session.
2. Establish the members who will participate. Since you want divergent views, make certain different voices are present to objectively represent possible solutions.

3. Establish a timeline that allows for everyone's input, time to reflect, and the criteria for making the decision.
4. During the meeting, create a dialogue where no idea is considered a bad idea for causing it to be discarded.
5. Don't allow reasons why the idea won't work at the initial stage.
6. Only after all the members have been presented do you begin analyzing the pros, cons, and options of each.
7. Require buy-in by all the members of the brainstorming session.

The last step in Gatty's version of brainstorming is questionable. In view of step #2 in the process, gaining buy-in of all members who originally represent the pros and cons of the matter at hand, is somewhat contentious. Goal #1 should be phased so as to take care of this contention. We would propose that the purpose of brainstorming is to gain a large number of new ideas and hope that some will be both unique and creative. That is, the purpose should focus on a generation of ideas rather than on their evaluation. Both the brainstorming members and their school organizations can consider the ideas and implement them as fits the case. The question that remains is, when will educators begin to implement the many beneficial practices available to them?

DECISION-MAKING AND EDUCATIONAL ADMINISTRATION

Decision-making pervades all other administration functions including planning, organizing, staffing, directing, coordinating, budgeting, reporting, and communicating. It has long been recognized as being at the heart of organization and administration. There have been two dominant sets of issues that have served to influence how decisions are made in organization. One set of issues arises from the universality of ongoing change as an urgent and overwhelming driving force in human affairs. Such developments as state and federal mandates, court rulings on desegregation, student inclusiveness, and criticism related to the lack of academic quality in school programs have changed the what, how, and when decisions relative to educational governance and local control of school programs.

In addition, the increasing rejection of the autocratic organizational ideas of the past and the rise of expectations of people at work that they will be involved in the decision-making process have given rise both to organizational conflict and to changes in "the way things are done around here." These changes have tended to pose a dilemma for school leaders who are faced with the need to make decisions quickly and the need for opening up participation in the process and empowering relevant people at all levels.

Research and empirical evidence have shown that participation in decision-making, and empowering relevant people at all levels, contributes to the health of the organization and to the quality of the decisions that are determined via group processes. As stated by Dan Griffiths and other leaders in the field of educational administration, "educational administration is decision-making." And, as noted previously in chapter 1, educational decision-making and critical thinking are inextricably related.

A LOOK AT PROBABLE CHANGES IN EDUCATIONAL PRACTICES

Educational practices that tend to be disappearing include the classroom with desks crowded together and a teacher in front departing knowledge. Rote learning and memory testing and the apparent singular focus on cognitive skills tend to lessen as social skills are given more attention. Practices that are being promoted but not always implemented educationally include the teacher serving as a guide for student learning rather than speaking from the platform of authority. Improving education is an objective of primary importance.

Changes in educational program provisions and practices are the "without which not" conditions for educational improvement. We contend that program provisions and practices without basic and empirical research support will likely fall short of expectations.

EDUCATION'S MISSING LINK: QUALITY RESEARCH PRACTICES

Suppose a miracle should occur whereby a cure for Alzheimer's disease was found through research programs. Within a very short time, practicing physicians around the world would have the medical program in place in hospitals and physicians' offices. Yet, if a research study were implemented on a learning method that doubled the student's achievement outcomes, school programs and faculties would most likely just continue what they were doing. This negative view reflects what education has been doing with research results in such areas as student retention in grade, class size, student learning styles, job satisfaction, administrative decision-making, and other educational program practices. Ongoing effective research continues to be education's primary inhibitor.

Give thought to a school or school district with which you are most familiar. Do either the individual school or the school district offices have an organized program research center? That is, does it have an educational research center that focuses on program content/practices, student learning, interventive pilot program results, and student achievement outcomes as opposed to conducting student retention data, dropout figures, teacher turnover statistics, and school enrollment projections?

To what extent is ongoing action research in evidence? In the absence of quality educational research programs at the state and local levels, schools are educating students in a vacuum, and quality school improvement has suffered as a result. Interventions are implemented in the absence of viable assessments and evaluations. We contend that the need for viable research is near the top of the reasons for the lack of improvement in education over the years. As John Dewey reportedly has stated, "If we teach today as we taught yesterday, we rob our children of tomorrow" (PROLOG, 2011, January 14).

WHAT IS NEEDED TO HELP MAKE EDUCATION IN AMERICA THE BEST IN THE WORLD?

Our contention has been that the quality of education that is provided for students today has great influence on their future success. What major factors tend to inhibit public school quality and what are the major success factors that have supported education in America? Norton (2019) identified six major factors that are inhibiting public school quality nationally. Such factors must be seriously attended and resolved if indeed today's education is to lead toward a student's future success. A leading inhibitor of public school quality, underscored by most every education authority in the nation, is that of inadequate financial support.

The contention that just putting more dollars into the education budget does not ensure a quality program for all students has some validity. Higher salaries for underperforming school personnel are not what is proposed. What must be achieved is a competitive compensation strategy that serves to attract and retain high-quality personnel into the educational profession. Empirical evidence demonstrates the fact that many high-quality persons who enter education leave the profession after only one year of service. Performance pay has not been popular within the teaching profession. Thus, mediocre teaching commonly receives the same salary as high-quality teaching. Years in service and the degree held determine compensation levels in the overwhelming majority of schools nationally.

The ability to pay for education varies greatly within the fifty states. Reports indicate that this statistic varies from 6 to 1 nationally. That is, some states are six times more able to meet education financial requirements than other states with low property evaluations. In any case, shortages of funding have inhibited the effectiveness of schools nationally in many ways. Various cuts in school programming, reductions in the school year, in some cases reducing the school week from five to four days, and the loss of many of the most qualified personnel are the result. Those groups and individuals that contend that a lack of funding is not a cause of failing education are failing themselves to understand that cuts in financial support can lead to reductions in student learning and ultimate achievement. We discuss Klein's and Rhee's recommendations for dealing with the financial problem in education later in the chapter.

A second inhibiting factor of education in America is the educational inequities that exist across states and school districts. Consider the situation where Johnny was born in Massachusetts and Mary was born in New Mexico. Neither child has any control relative to their place of birth or, if their parents continue to reside in the respective states, the public school system that they will attend. However, we referred to the WalletHub study of public school quality (2018) rankings which named Massachusetts as being of the highest quality and New Mexico as being last in the quality rankings. Should it be surprising that Massachusetts per pupil support for education is near the highest nationally and New Mexico's is among the lowest? Equality in education remains a myth.

Equal opportunity for a quality education has been among the highest pronouncements in the American democracy since the nation was established. As yet, this pronouncement has yet to be fulfilled. We recommend reading the book, *The White House and Education through the Years: U.S. Presidents' Views and Significant Educational Contributions* (Norton, 2018), for further views on this topic. For example, three selected statements by former president Barack Obama on the topic are as follows:

- "Every young person in America deserves a world-class education. We've got an obligation to give it to them."
- "It's not enough to train today's workforce. We must also prepare tomorrow's workforce by guaranteeing every child access to a world-class education."
- "The agenda starts with education. A highly-educated and skilled workforce will be the key not only to individual opportunity, but to the overall success of our country."

A third primary inhibitor is the *decreasing of local control of K–12 education*. Historically, local school education has been considered as a federal concern, a state responsibility, and a local function. Although each state is given the primary control of education, the states have delegated the implementation of school programming to the individual school districts. The primary characteristics of such local control is vested in the governance policies and administrative regulations that set forth the purposes and the methods for carrying out valid and relevant education at the local level. Those closest to the scene have been considered as the best ones to understand the most appropriate programs for meeting the needs and interests of students in the school-community.

Unfortunately, the requirements for serving on local school boards are not only limited but have little or nothing to do with the requirements of the work of school board members who are selected to govern the school programs. School board policies, those statements that set forth the primary school goals and objectives, are seldom in the hands of school board members and the professional staff. Rather, the policy manuals for school operations are determined primarily by boilerplate policy manuals outsourced to state school board associations. Administrative and faculty involvement in policy development is minimal at best.

In addition to the reduction in policy development, school boards are strapped increasingly by federal and state mandates for program operations, and the courts are increasingly involved in rulings as to how the school district is to perform its program duties. The loss of local involvement in policy recommendations and their adoption also reduces the engagement of the school personnel in determining best school practices but also in the actual implementation of directives set forth by the outside sources. As a result, it is common for school governance policy/regulation manuals to sit on the shelves in teachers' classrooms gathering dust.

"When local school board control is weakened, external forces tend to enter into the business of the school. Local school-community purposes of education give way to external mandates and curricular program requirements that must be implemented if certain external funds are to be appropriated" (Norton, 2019, p. 9). In addition, local community interest and the support of internal faculty in school affairs commonly are reduced.

Poor student academic performance serves as the fourth primary inhibitor of school education in America. Pros and cons concerning the quality of education in America have existed throughout history. In fact, it seems impossible to identify an educational program or practice that is not the target of ongoing controversy. Charter schools, standardized testing, student retention, prayer in schools, sex education, teacher compensation, open classrooms, curricular provisions, and teacher load are among the many other educational issues that are being encountered in contemporary education today.

The foregoing kinds of problems noted above lead to other major problems concerning the ability to establish high-quality school programs nationally. Inability to attract and retain high-quality education personnel ranks high on the list of inhibiting problems and represents the fifth major inhibitor of K–12 education. Contemporary problems such as high levels of teacher turnover and the resulting loss of program stability, the poor quality of teacher and administrator preparation programs, and the historical instructional strategy that centers on memorization and regurgitation of knowledge are representative of related educational problems.

The sixth major inhibitor of local school education is the flawed organizational procedures and mismanagement within many school districts in America. We noted previously the basic need for improving local school control and the importance of completely revising the requirements of school board membership. Organizational Development strategies are vacant in many local school districts. As a result, much time and effort are given to after-the-fact pending problems.

Effective leadership preparation programs for potential administrators are wanting. In short, an entirely new program for administrative preparation is needed. This matter of the need for a major revision of administrator preparation programs could well be included in the list of primary educational inhibitors. In short, university preparation programs must be founded on research-based knowledge that serves not only to help resolve educational problems but provides the knowledge and skills necessary for dealing with needed program changes before major problems exist.

MAJOR SUCCESS FACTORS OF PUBLIC EDUCATION THAT NEED TO BE EXTENDED

In spite of the fact that serious education inhibiting factors are evidenced in contemporary education, several positive outcomes need to be further extended throughout school districts. The efforts to include all students in K–12 education programs is positive practice #1. In the early 1960s, few school districts nationally had inclusive educational opportunities for students with special needs. Later, in the 1980s, the effort to include all students in K–12 school programs was in place. Special education classes for students with special needs, especially those with learning difficulties, were established. Special education programs for teachers were implemented and the services for students with special needs other than mental retardation were implemented in most schools nationally.

Today's local special education programs include students with: physical disabilities, attention deficit disorder, neurological impairments, serious emotional disturbances, speech and language impairments, autism/pervasive development disorder, Asperger's Syndrome, bipolar disorder, blind and vision disorder, cerebral palsy, mental retardation, dyslexia, homelessness, Tourette syndrome, and others. In addition, student special services such as occupational therapy, rehabilitation counseling, social services, home schools, and others are effectively in place. These educational provisions are to be highly applauded and extended as needed throughout local school programs nationally.

Teacher preparation programs have come a long way since the teachers' institutes were established by Henry Barnard in the early 1840s designed to focus on the basics, globes, and "school keeping." Some high school graduates served as teachers in K–6 schools nationally. By 1870, the two-year normal school for teachers became prominent. The majority of elementary school teachers held the two-year teaching degree, while secondary teachers tended to hold a four-year college degree. Today, many teachers hold master's degrees although there has been a tendency to earn that degree in educational administration. A master's degree in administration is outside the teaching specialty of most school personnel but commonly moves the individual up the ladder on the single-salary compensation scale.

HIGH SCHOOL GRADUATION STATISTICS

High school graduation statistics have shown an improvement in the number of students who graduate from high school. Although the approximate 80 percent graduation rate has improved over the years, rates of graduation for various racial groups continue to be unsatisfactory. Various reports also indicate that from 60 percent to 80 percent of high school graduates are now entering college, although statistics for continuation in higher education are not impressive. In any case, we view the success statistic for high school graduation as a success statistic. More students and their parents are viewing education as an important objective; both the student and the nation benefit by these positive results.

The production of social mobility and attention to affective skills, in the views of many authorities, are most important for the realization of future success. Effective collaboration, group cooperation, and civil behavior are essential for successful living today and tomorrow. Some authorities and many educational personnel have pointed to the paramount importance of social maturity. Affective skills are demonstrated by the characteristics of caring, communication skills, cooperative/collaborative, commitment, enthusiasm, fairness, kindness, creativity, compassion, respectful, creativity, and others.

One can point to a number of public school problems that tend to set aside any arguments that social maternity is present in our schools today. Such characteristics as bullying, student violence, lack of student discipline, disobedience, apathy, discourtesy, and other unfortunate social behaviors are identified as problems in all too many school reports. Such behaviors are highly inhibiting in professional activities where cooperation, collaboration, critical thinking, and teamwork are essential. We contend that improvement of student social skills and civil behaviors should indeed be one of the public school's important purposes now and in all the years ahead.

Nevertheless, many schools and school children are demonstrating the kinds of social skills that are of primary importance. We note a humorous experience in one middle school in Nebraska. A district curriculum coordinator entered the middle school and was walking through the hall toward the school office when he came across a school student. As the coordinator approached the student, the student commented, "Good afternoon, sir, may I help you find someone?" The coordinator had visited the school's principal's office before on several occasions and knew the location of that office quite well. However, he answered the student, "I thank you, but I do know that the school office is down the hall and to the right." He thanked the student once again and moved on to the school office.

When the coordinator reached the school office, the school principal, Kathryn Scott, was on hand to meet him. He knew the principal and her sense of humor quite well. The coordinator smiled and said hello and then told the principal how impressed he was by the young student's courtesy and his willingness to help in getting to the school office.

Well, responded Principal Scott, "We are always up and ready to tell visitors where to go!"

POST-CHAPTER QUIZ/REVIEW

1. Critical thinking commonly is defined as the language used by individuals who always tend to be negative about new interventions that might make changes in the way things are done in the school system. True____ or False____
2. Since information reportedly will be available immediately via various technological means, problem-solving skills are lessening in their importance in present and future organizations. True____ or False____
3. Group decision-making, although being emphasized in the predictions for the future by both individuals and groups, will be reduced in its importance due to the continuous emphasis on specialists within the organization. True____ or False____
4. The single-salary schedule used by the large majority of school districts in America will continue to be in place the next decade due to its effectiveness in fostering equity among professional personnel in education. True____ or False____
5. Historically, education has been viewed as a federal responsibility due to its mention in the Tenth Amendment of the United States Constitution. True____ or False____
6. The requirements for local school board membership must be examined and revised. The rigidity of membership requirements has inhibit-

ed the ability for many local citizens to apply for the position. True____ or False____
7. Local control of school programs has finally been achieved due mainly to boards' primary attention given to the internal development and adoption of governance policies and administrative regulations. True____ or False____
8. The record of local school districts in providing for the needs of students with special needs reveals evidence that education equity is being overlooked. True____ or False____
9. High school graduation statistics have revealed an improvement in the percent of students graduating from the nation's schools. True____ or False____
10. Student success in the future has been viewed as being dependent on a greater emphasis on cognitive knowledge and skills with social skills being left most exclusively at the doorstep of students' parents. True____ or False____

ANSWERS TO THE CHAPTER'S POST-QUIZ

Question #1 is *False*. Critical thinking skills have been named as one of the most important skills that schools should be teaching as opposed to rote learning and regurgitation of facts. The chapter underscores the important relationship of change to problem solving, wise decision-making, critical thinking, collaboration, and creativity. Critical thinking is the "without which not" of effective decision-making and effective change.

Question #2 is *False*. On the contrary, problem-solving skills leads the list of those skills that are needed in contemporary education and loom highly important for effective living in the future. One key point of the chapter was the fact that high on the list of expectations for school leaders is that problem solving is their primary work responsibility. One authority was noted for his contention that the best school leaders are the best problem solvers. We tend to agree with this contention but believe that the best school leaders have the foresight to plan and implement positive changes that eliminate and/or reduce the effects of pending problems that any organization is bound to confront.

Question #3 is *False*. We consider the answer to this question as being false since various authority sources contend that services of specialists, as we have known them, will be reduced due to the thrust toward group involvements in decision-making matters and the trend toward major collaboration activities nationally and internationally worldwide. That is, the ideas of a wide variety of human resources serve to enhance critical thinking, the implementation of beneficial decision models, and a national and international collaborative process as opposed to a more singular specialist approach.

Question #4 is *False*. It might not be a big surprise, but the single-salary schedule might still be in place in many school districts by the year 2030. First and perhaps foremost, other compensation methods in education, such as performance pay, are not supported by "powerful" teacher association groups. In addition, other major education problems stand in the way of monetary changes. Lack of funding support, changes in the projected job roles of teachers, the relative acceptance of the single-salary method by the professional teaching staff and school-community, and the lack of other compensation alternatives, other than performance-pay, tend to serve as primary inhibitors of changes in compensation methods in education. The question needing additional thinking is, "Why do performance pay and other compensation methods appear to work satisfactorily in higher education and numerous major business and industrial organization and not in education?"

Question #5 is *False*. Of course, it is widely known that education is not mentioned in the United States of America Constitution. As the Tenth Amendment states, the powers not delegated to the United States by the Constitution, nor prohibited by it, are reserved to the states respectively or to the people. However, Article 1, Section 8, of the U.S. Constitution states that Congress can collect taxes, pay debts, provide for the common defense and general welfare, but it must be uniform over all the states. We mention Article 1, Section 8, since it includes the words "for the common defense and general welfare." The general welfare clause has been used by Congress to enter education programs at the local level since they can be viewed as "being good for the general welfare" of the nation.

Question #6 is *False*. Although it is true that, in our opinion, the requirements for membership on local school boards should be reviewed, it is not due to the fact that they are too stringent. On the contrary, school board membership requirements are flawed in that none of the present requirements relate importantly to the actual work requirements of the role.

If school boards are to continue as governance bodies in America, a relevant list of school board member qualifications must be drafted that reflects the knowledge, experience, and skills required by school board members in the role.

Question # 7 is *False*. At present, governance policy and administrative regulations for K–12 education commonly are boilerplate productions by state school board associations or other external resources. The most important responsibility of school board members is school program governance. Policies and regulations drafted, approved, and implemented at the local school level serve not only the internal school programs but serve to implement and retain local control of the school-community programs. Boilerplate policies set forth by external agencies find themselves on the shelves of classroom teachers gathering dust. Commitment to the policies and engagement in their implementation are missing. The lack of personnel engagement, along with community member input, militates against the effectiveness of program purposes and important administrative performance.

Question #8 is *False*. On the contrary, the positive work in the area of special education by local school districts has been exemplary. Special needs services have continually been expanded and improved. Efforts to include special needs children in the regular school programs and activities are to be commended as well.

Question #9 is *True*. Although graduation statistics for students of different races and ethnicities differ, the overall graduation statistics show an improvement which approximates an 80 percent high school graduation achievement. In addition, a larger percentage of high school graduates are entering college.

Question #10 is *False*. Knowledge and skill characteristics certainly are included in the many predictions for success in the future. However, many authorities point to the paramount importance of social skills as being of prime importance in the future. The characteristics of collaboration, cooperation, communication, group decision-making, and effective problem solving nationally and internationally, underscore the importance of social skills that include caring, fairness, kindness, respect, and teamwork among the human races.

KEY CHAPTER IDEAS AND RECOMMENDATIONS

- Changes in the national workforce whereby organizations will have teams of employees collaborating with different offices across the planet hold many implications for educational program practices in America. Both social and academic knowledge and skills continue to be of paramount importance.
- Critical thinking, as opposed to rote learning, will be needed for problem solving among the changes that will inevitably occur over the years.
- Problem solving will continue to be a necessary skill for education personnel and thus must be given specific attention in preparation programs for educational leaders.
- Problem solving is a primary responsibility of educational leaders and should be viewed as opportunities for program improvement.
- If education is to be improved, basic and empirical research must become a reality in the programs of local schools and school districts in America.
- Today is tomorrow in relation to educational purposes and outcomes. Therefore, the various inhibiting factors that deter educational success must be confronted and resolved. Educational research, a present weak-

ness in educational practices, must become a major priority within the local schools and school districts nationally.
- The success factors of today's educational programs must continue in practice as well as being continually extended and improved.
- The production of social mobility and attention to the affective skills of caring, compassion, and cooperation are of paramount importance for the realization of future success for all students.
- Local control of education has been eroded due to ongoing interventions by the state and federal agencies. Further attention must be placed on the ways and means that policies and regulations are developed and implemented at the local school level.
- Boilerplate policies, completed by external agencies, inhibit the authority of local school boards and lessen the involvement of school personnel to develop and implement local school governance.

DISCUSSION QUESTIONS

1. Assume that you are the superintendent of schools for the Wymore School District and meeting with a group of community business leaders. One businessperson at the meeting stood and stated, "The school board election is near and three new board members are to be elected." Just what is the primary role of a school board member and what qualifications are required? Set forth your response to the individual's question.
2. Explain the meaning of critical thinking and what it means relative to educational program practices. Why is there much thought being given to critical thinking in relation to student success in the decades to come?
3. At a meeting of your school board, one board member asks, "Why are we giving so much thought to the social activities in our program in our schools? Isn't the pressure being placed on the low performance of students in our academic subject?" You are a principal in the school district and the school superintendent turns to you for a response. Take time to write a brief response that you might give at the meeting.
4. At a local after-school faculty meeting, the conversation has focused on the inhibiting factors that are being encountered in the school's everyday practices. One teacher commented, "Why are we dealing with such inhibitors as lack of school funds, teacher turnover, and school dropouts? Most every one of the so-called inhibitors are outside of our control. Let the parents and members of the school-community solve these problems. We have no control over them!" As school principal, set forth your response. Avoid stating answers such

as, "Well, that's just the way it is," or "All we can do is the best we can." Your critical thinking is needed here.
5. Give serious thought to the chapter's considerations and the implications for the future of education by 2030. What topics or recommendations of most importance in your case come to mind? For example, considerable attention was given to the importance of collaboration in the future. Consider collaboration and other characteristics as they come into play for future student success.

REFERENCES

Bombeck, W. (1974). Group vs. individual decision-making. An unpublished doctoral dissertation. Arizona State University. Department of Educational Supervision and Policy Studies. Tempe, AZ.

Gatty, A. (2019, February 6). Tag Archives: Brainstorming, business decision-making improves with brainstorming. From the web: https://www.strategicpeoplesolutions.com/posts/business-decision-making-improves-with-brainstorming/

Llopis, G. (2013, November 4). The 4 most effective ways leaders solve problems. *Forbes*.

Nichols, J. R. (2015, November 5). 7 skills students will always need. *Teachthought: The Future of Learning*.

Norton, M. S. (2015). *The Changing Landscape of School Leadership: Recalibrating the School Principalship*. Lanham, MD: Rowman & Littlefield.

Norton, M. S. (2018). *The White House and Education through the Years: U.S. Presidents and Significant Educational Contributions*. Lanham, MD: Roman & Littlefield.

Norton, M. S. (2019). *Making our Schools the Best in the World: Re-Imagining Education Outside the Proverbial Box*. Lanham, MD: Rowman & Littlefield.

PROLOG. (2011, January 14). *John Dewey Quotes*. From the web: https://www.bing.com/videos/search?q=Gatty962C+2015percent2C+improving+decision+making&go=Search&qs=ds&form=OBVR

Williams, J. (2017, February 9). What changes in the workforce mean for the future of workplace design. *Work Design Magazine*. From the web: https://www.workdesign.com/2017/02/changes-workforce-mean-future-workplace-design/

Chapter Three

K–12 Education and the Future

PRIMARY CHAPTER GOAL

To examine the many predictions of current and ongoing practices by teachers, administrators, various groups, and research teams relative to the status of schools and education for preparing students for the decades ahead.

PREDICTING THE FUTURE

An examination of the numerous sources that have set forth predictions regarding the status of education in the decades ahead collectively provides an "amazing" picture of educational changes that are no less than "unbelievable." However, when it comes to research information or just how certain future predictions will be implemented in school programs, this information is missing. Predictions tend to remind us of a session with a fortune-teller; the "client" is commonly fascinated with the stated possibilities, but the predictions just seem to fade away.

A look at the volume of literature on the topic of education's future gives one some idea as to the present thinking of education's predicted future. Several examples of publications that have projected views for the future of K–12 education are presented in the following section. We site these references and set forth one brief citation that includes the "thinking" of the author on the topic at hand.

1. *Preparing Your Students for the Challenges of Tomorrow* (J. Willis, 2014, August 20).

    "Teach collaboration as a value and skill Set: Students today need new skills for the coming century that will make them ready to collab-

orate with others on a global level. 'Whatever they do, we can expect their work to include finding creative solutions to emerging challenges'" (p. 2).
2. *Schools of 2030: No Grades, No Exams, No Teachers* (K. Houshmand, 2018, May 11).

   "Among the most frequent proposals . . . was that of 'stage-based not age-based' learning. This would mean getting rid of grades 9–12 and replacing it [sic] with a project-based system. Students would learn as they progressed through the materials, not held back or moved forward because of their age" (p. 2).
3. *How do we prepare today's learners for tomorrow's jobs?* (Hanover Research, 2014).

   "Automation, along with globalization, leaves many workers with an uncertain future" (p. 1). One study forecasts the contention that ten workers are in jobs presently that have an uncertainty about their future.
4. *Preparing for Today and Tomorrow* (Eisner, E. W., 2003–2004).

   "If an unknown future is not a sound basis on which to plan curriculum and instruction, then what is? From my perspective, we can best prepare students for the future by enabling them to deal effectively with the present" (p. 1).
5. *American Education in 2030* (Hoover Institution [2014]).

   "Schools will no longer manage all schools, and assign students to schools. Instead, 'portfolio school districts' will manage the mix of schools to meet the needs of all local students, hiring many different school providers, some from local providers—colleges, teacher groups, museums, and professional school management organizations—and some from statewide national organizations. Some schools will rely heavily on online instruction and employ few teachers. To promote improvement, portfolio school districts will hold all to the same student performance standard" (stated by Paul T. Hill, p. 2).
6. *Public Schools 2025: A Vision for the Future* (Pappafotopoulos, 2011, July 23).

   "In 2025, I can visualize a school that is more like a community center, open year round from 8 am til 8 pm, and staffed by teams of professional educators who are each 'on call' for 6–8 hours each day. The elimination of classroom grades will do away with what Charles Taylor Kerchner labels as 'batch-process learning,' to be replaced by learning—more choices and more challenges for students" (p. 1).
7. *The Future of Continuing Education Can Be Found in K–12 Classrooms* (T. Grzybowski, 2018).

   Four teachers were interviewed, and five fundamental shifts/themes in today's educational environment: Moving away from a defined curriculum, teacher and student roles have changed, students have more choice and voice in their own learning, technology is a great facilitator, and assessments have changed in that testing methods have started to evolve to more accurately reflect true proficiency using application-based assessments.

The following discussions in the chapter center on projected features in education in relation to structure and facilities, curricular design, human resources, needed work skills, and improved financial support. Although education is commonly referenced as the most important influence for maintaining a democratic society and giving each and every individual an opportunity for a successful life, it seems to sit on the sidelines waiting for change to happen rather than being in front for making positive changes in the best interests of the citizenry.

Follower-ship rather than leadership is most prevalent. Shouldn't education be in a leadership position in effecting change that meets the needs of society? Is the statement "Change has brought about new needs to do something differently in education," or should the statement be "Education has brought about new knowledge and skills that should be implemented in society for the purpose of improving life"?

FUTURE PROJECTIONS: SCHOOL BUILDING CONSTRUCTION

Visions set forth for school building constructions range from common classroom facilities with indications of modern technology updates to large community educational campuses to changeable/portable classroom facilities that stand ready for providing a needed learning environment for the day's learning objectives, to no school building or classrooms at all; online home learning is available when desired or required. For example, the winning architectural design set forth by Future Proofing Schools (2019) featured a flexible modern design system that can be configured to create a building system that adapts to specific requirements such as site, climate, and learning outcomes.

The winning concept was judged as being both sophisticated and simple with adaptable and transportable space. Contemporary thinking has given much thought to school culture and climate. However, projected thinking on school learning climate in the future gives serious thought to climate in relation to school construction and facilities; that is the learning environment.

The overall visions for future school building construction commonly express characteristics that provide various learning "spaces," safety features, relocatable classrooms, learning areas that utilize both internal/external environments around the building, flexibility of learning spaces over and above rational, workable, arrangements of classrooms. Various pods which encourage students to take greater responsibility for their own learning are provided via the creation of project pods, breakout pods, social pods, and outdoor spaces that provide the opportunity for students to learn from nature (from the web, see LAVA in references).

General features of educational structures must give serious thought to other design features. For example, provisions such as student engagement/ collaboration, digital backpacks, personalized learning, independent study, and extended learning schedules call for new technological utilization in educational settings. Some needed, but not necessarily new, features must be brought into the classroom facilities discussion relative to their importance for facilitating effective learning.

Future school construction must give serious attention to the related environments in which learning is to take place. Empirical evidence has demonstrated the advantages of natural lighting in schools. A study group in one state set forth several significant claims for natural lighting in schools. The study group that consisted of school principals and teachers expressed the opinion that natural lighting tended to improve the positive effects of student learning. Such factors as student attention, student feelings of security, and alertness were better in an environment of natural lighting.

In any case, classroom climates should facilitate group interaction, collaboration, and ongoing communication. Classroom colors and lighting placements are being given newly deserved attention as well. Studies have shown for years that natural lighting is best for student achievement rates. Some florescent lighting has been found to cause a reflection that hinders reading words on paper or on the chalkboard. Highly lit environments have been found to improve student learning. In any case, rethinking the learning environments for students requires the rethinking of the colors of the learning environment and the quality of the lighting in which learning is to take place.

A facility research unit must come into play if and when such climate factors are on the table. Will the construction company be highly knowledgeable of the classroom color schemes for purposes of facilitating learning? What about the involvement of classroom teacher and school administrative leaders? These users of the school facilities most often are ignored and/or overlooked when it comes to building models and interior qualifications for facilitating student learning. After all, they have had little or no preparation for giving direction to school facility planning. How are educators to be involved in the decisions relative to the environments in which student learning is to take place?

At the far end of school facility predictions for the future is a classroom that doesn't actually exist. The thought of gaining knowledge and skill outside and away from a physical classroom is proposed by various authorities more frequently in the literature. Learning and teaching could come from most anywhere. In any case, it seems quite possible that learning can be motivated and improved outside the four walls of the traditional classroom.

The oft-stated contention that the student has the personal motivation and wisdom to determine what is in his or her best interests is in need of serious pilot study and assessment. Just how is this revolutionary strategy being practiced in any school system today? And, if it is, where is the research that tells us that the best learning is that which is determined by the students and their ideas as to what learning is needed and in their best interests?

Nevertheless, some persons are of the opinion that "almost everything is in place for such a system now. The main thing stopping it is that we're stuck in an old-mind model of what education looks like. We believe it has to be classroom based in one location, etc. Once we bust out of that model and are open to exploring the alternatives, amazing transformations to our educational system are going to happen" (in Fudin [2011, November 15], as commented by Anthony Papillion).

It appears to be somewhat problematic if the predictions of full-scale homeschooling come to pass. How are the characteristics of collaboration to be implemented? How is the increased need and use of personal technology to be funded and installed? Ask most any teacher if they ever have been asked about the color that they would like to have in their classroom. How are lighting and color schemes to be controlled and by whom? How is 24/7 learning to be implemented in a homeschooling environment? Far-reaching predictions of education's future are seldom accompanied by rational strategies/methods for funding them. Perhaps an effort to manufacture magic wands to achieve such ends will serve the stated purposes.

We address the solution of home schooling and other future conditions in education in the following chapter 4. In the meantime, Bushmaker and others (2015, July/August) lend the following advice: "To prepare our current and future students for the colleges and careers of tomorrow, we must be keenly aware of the evolution of educational design today. A strong facilities assessment and creative planning can lead to the creation of a truly 21st-century learning environment while building in flexibility to accommodate an unforeseen future" (p. 11). To learn how this advice is achieved, contact Bushmaker, Leed, and Koehler at Hoffman Planning Design & Construction, Inc., in Appleton, Wisconsin; email: rkoehler@hoffman.net.

Good luck!

WHAT ABOUT EDUCATION, THE SCHOOL'S CURRICULUM, AND THE CLASSROOMS IN 2030?

Finding predictions for education by the year 2030 is not a problem. The problem is trying to summarize the myriad of predictions that are being proliferated. Various individuals, forums, survey results, authority assessment conferences, and a dozen other discussion groups have given their opinions as to what K–12 education will "look like" in the next decade. An opinion is commonly defined as a view or judgment about something, not necessarily based on fact or knowledge. It is a judgment, viewpoint of a statement that is not conclusive.

THE 2030 CURRICULUM IN THE NOWALLS SCHOOL DISTRICT IN LAFAYETTE

Give serious thought to the school curriculum in the decades ahead before you set forth your ideas about the schools' programming. Sarah Fudin did so in 2011 (November 15) and was immediately met with "criticisms" by twenty-two responders. For example, one responder to Fudin's projections expressed the opinion that, "How is this helpful? For every one brilliant entrepreneur this system develops, it will generate a thousand young adults with no marketable skills" (p. 6). Fudin's future classroom list for 2021 was not all that "far out." She conservatively stated that, "classrooms will be paperless, classrooms will cater to more individualized instruction based on a student's passions, communication will vastly improve and new learning spaces will pop up—no more individual desks" (p. 2).

When it comes to curricular program provisions, future projections for school programs tend to be much more different than those of today. In any case, we do not see the hands of the state or federal agencies being removed from "mandates" regarding what is to be taught, who is to teach it, and how it is to be presented. In the following section, the projections for school curriculum provisions are discussed. To assume that parents are willing and able to assume the educational program requirements for their child seems to be a bit out of reach even for the year 2030. In 2019, for example, only 4.5 percent of students in K–12 public and private schools were in homeschooling.

Contemporary curricula of K–12 schools most commonly list a variety of courses under the headings of science, mathematics, social science, and practical skills. Since the programming of learning experiences in the year 2030 varies from open classrooms, to online classes, to homeschooling, and to no classrooms, attempts to set forth a listing of related courses in any one area of learning are highly probable. Future course curricular discussion most commonly focus on affective and cognitive skills. Rather than having a particular cognitive skill being emphasized in any one "course" offering, recommendations focus on having each skill be taken seriously in each "learning experience" being pursued.

Common terms often mentioned in discussions of future curriculum development include digital learning, flipped learning, stage-based learning, mobile learning, social learning networks, cloud computing, learning analytics, E-Portfolios, open content, personalized learning environment, augmented reality, virtual laboratories, blended learning environments, and other twenty-first-century skills. Hanover Research (2014, October) has identified trends that are likely to influence educational practices in America's schools in the years ahead. Several of these trends have been selected for definitional purposes in the following section. Each trend holds specific implications for addressing the school's curricular program and the provisions for implementing the concepts of the trend in practice.

Mobile learning includes education or training by means of portable devices such as smart phones and computers. It is flexible and readily available to students most everywhere. Unfortunately, like many computer devices, mobile learning has its limitations. The rapid changes in mobile devices tend to lead to problems of outdatedness. In addition, certain problems regarding cultural issues have led to the prevention of their use in some settings.

Virtual and remote laboratories are programs that use web resources. A virtual lab is based on software to simulate the lab environment. On the other hand, the remote lab allows the student to carry out experiments with the actual instruments.

Flipped classrooms constitute an instructional change that reverses the traditional arrangement by delivering instructional content often online, outside the classroom. First, students prepare to participate in the classroom activities. In one sense, they do their homework first. During class, students practice the applications of the concepts with feedback from the guiding teachers and perhaps others. Afterward, students check their understanding and extend their learning as best fits the case. The teacher becomes an instructional guide as opposed to a deliverer of knowledge, although he or she will spend time working individually with students.

Open content is when the material is available for copying without need to gain permission. The copy may be revised freely. Open education resources can include full courses, course materials, modules, textbooks, videos, tests, software, and other tools and techniques used to support access to knowledge. The point is this: knowledge and related resources are projected to be readily available to all students regardless of their educational status.

Personalized learning environments serve to meet each child's needs and interests wherever they are learning and to help them meet their potential toward the goal of educating the whole child. Personalized learning takes place inside and outside the classroom. Student needs drive the design of the learning environment, including the use of space, schedules, technology, and talent. Each child gets a learning plan based on what he or she knows and how the child learns best.

E-Portfolios are an electronic version of the traditional portfolio that was a collection of items on paper, created by a student to represent his or her learning progress or best work. E-Portfolios are digital collections that are typically available through the internet with access at anytime and anywhere. Paperless classrooms are predicted for future classrooms commonly throughout contemporary literature.

Social learning networks are means whereby students can use online networking to create portfolios that are available to peers and others for project-based networking. Collaboration with others for purposes of cooperative learning is facilitated. Hanover Research (2014) describes Edmodo that provides students with the tools to collaborate with one another. Student progress can be monitored by the teacher and other instructional activities can also be used. Reportedly, Edmodo had more than seventeen million users at the time this citation was published. Nimbus is another product in which teachers, parents, and students can collaborate and build critical thinking and problem-solving skills. Curricular topics and other program activities can be discussed cooperatively using Nimbus.

WHAT ABOUT PROGRAM SUBJECT CONTENT FOR EDUCATION IN THE FUTURE?

Contemporary curriculum content commonly has been viewed as the courses offered in the areas of mathematics, science, English, fine arts, vocational education, and industrial arts. Future projections for the curriculum tend to focus more specifically on the knowledge and skills that students need to be successful in life. As Eisner (2003–2004) has stated, "The unknowable future is not a sound basis on which to plan curriculum . . . if an unknowable future is not a sound basis on which to plan curriculum and instruction, then what is? From my perspective, we can best prepare students for the future by enabling them to deal effectively with the present" (p. 1). In this sense, today is tomorrow. Preparation for the future is best achieved by assuring that each student experiences a relevant and effective education today.

Discussions of the school curriculum in the future most often criticize the practice of memorizing facts and figures and then being able to recite and/or recall them from memory. Since the advances of technology have fostered the ease of gaining information instantly, such a result has placed new emphasis on being able to use "computer knowledge" effectively. That is, school programming should give special emphasis to helping the student develop the affective and cognitive skills that are needed to communicate and utilize the processes of effective communication, collaboration, and cooperation with other individuals and groups.

The critical skills of thinking and problem solving were discussed in chapter 1. The workplace today, and we believe for the future, "demands" one's ability to work effectively with teams that are not only within one's organization but are more commonly completed with individuals and groups that are external to the organization to which one belongs. As soon as the team that is collaborating on a problem comes up with the best solution, this team is dissolved and the worker finds himself or herself working with a new group on a new problem. What special skills are needed in this environment?

The special skills of oral and written communication, problem solving, critical thinking, collaboration, agility and adaptability, initiative, assessing and analyzing, and curiosity and imagination were discussed in previous chapters. In the following sections of the chapter, other crucial skills of high importance for continued success in the future include judgment, initiative and entrepreneurship, leadership, individualism, personal service, self-cognizance, and others. We contend that such skills can be taught, improved, and practiced though the curriculum of the school. Are such skills part of the school's curriculum? Indeed, they are when we are considering the school's program essentials for the future. The individual skills are directly curriculum related in the sense that they must be addressed in every program course rather than being a course within themselves.

HOW THE CONTEMPORARY SKILLS ARE DEVELOPED IN K–12 EDUCATION PROGRAMS

We contend that the important skills of critical thinking, decision-making, problem solving, creativity, agility, judgment, creativity, and others can indeed be developed in students as early as preschool programs through grade 12. In the following section, several affective and cognitive skills have been selected for consideration in relation to various strategies/provisions for promoting their development in students. A skill such as critical thinking is developed in relation to other courses such as social science, science, and English literature.

A mentor or teacher, for example, might ask students why critical thinking is important. After gaining some thoughts about what critical thinking entails and why it is important, a discussion of what the student thinks he or she knows about a political or social matter is brought up for clarification. The teacher asks students the question, "How do you know what you think you know about the question at hand?" The teacher uses key questions to engage a student toward considering new ways of thinking about the matter at hand. What are the primary problems or issues related to the topic? What are the primary issues related to the present solution and what basic research or experience is available for our consideration? What options are available in answer to the question at hand? What facts serve to support the present position on the matter? Which solution among the probable solutions is best supported by the evidence that has been revealed?

The skill of judgment also comes into play in determining the final solution. Judgment is the ability to make considered opinions or come to sensible solutions based on careful thought. In preparation of students for success in the future, educational leaders must implement those critical thinking skills that prepare students for judicially observing and questioning the world around them. Focusing on rote learning and simply "reciting" their recollections via a flawed testing strategy is unsatisfactory.

It is wise for us to be reminded that the so-called problem being faced is probably never totally resolved. What most commonly happens is that certain "pieces" of the problem/matter at hand are determined and implemented in the school's program. Other pieces fall through the cracks of ever-changing times and may or may not ever come back to the surface for further attention. Nevertheless, a solution is reached and it too most likely will be in need of readjustment; new challenges/changes take place and present new issues with new needs.

As has been noted previously, because new evidence has shown that participation in decision-making and the empowerment of relevant people at all levels contribute both to the health of the organization and to the quality of the decisions implemented. More attention has been given to participative decision-making and various concerns relative to group processes. It should be no surprise that the factors of collaboration, cooperation, and worldwide communication have loomed as being of paramount importance in contemporary and future educational program practices.

SERVING STUDENTS BY FOSTERING SKILL SETS THAT PREPARE THEM FOR THE FUTURE

Willis (2014, August 20) set forth six challenges/opportunities that give guidance for preparing students for a successful future. We cite Willis's work herein but recommend your full reading of the article which you can locate by checking the references in this chapter. Willis understands that administration requires preparation toward the mastery of standards that are foundational to effective administrative leadership. However, she asks the question, "What can you promote to be sure they (students) are equipped with the skill sets they will need to take on the challenges and opportunities that we can't yet even imagine?" (p. 1). Her response to this key question is set forth in chapter 4.

We enter Willis's first recommendation for preparing students for what they are likely to face in the years and decades to come. Note that Willis's recommendations were set forth approximately six years ago in 2014. Teaching collaboration as a value and skill set was Willis's recommendation #1. She indeed was on target in her stated views that "students of today (2014) need new skills for the coming century that will make them ready to collaborate with others on the global level" (p. 2).

In 1999, a major study of the status of collaboration in the preparation programs for school leaders was completed. The purpose of the study was to ascertain the status of collaborative activities between/among preparation programs in UCEA universities and several constituencies such as business groups and other administrator organizations nationally. It was assumed that the results of the study would provide information relative to the extent to which educational administration programs were involving other individuals and groups in the preparation of school leaders. Forty-six UCEA member institutions participated in the study.

Six specific collaborative activities were listed for the respondents' consideration with an opportunity for listing additional activities. Each of the six collaboration entries centered primarily on collaboration that took place between department faculty personnel and their students. External collaboration with local community members, business leaders, or outreach globally was not in evidence.

There is an increasing activity of global online collaboration. Interactions concerning curricular program objectives are being advocated and initially practiced today. As a result, cultural relations and mutual understandings are positively enhanced. We now hear talk about building a collaborative school. How is this objective to be achieved and why is this objective important for helping students better prepare for the future?

WHAT DOES IT TAKE TO HAVE EFFECTIVE COLLABORATION?

What is meant by effective collaboration? Most commonly, the answer given to the question is the communication that the school has with others in the school-community. In fact, effective collaboration necessitates broader and deeper program activities. Effective collaboration, as we view it here, is achieved when the results of two or more members of a team are greater than what might be accomplished by individual members on their own. In a collaborative arrangement, school members work together to accomplish a shared purpose. Collaboration requires working together, learning together, sharing knowledge, and positive working relationships.

It is an authentic arrangement that presents opportunities for professional learning, sharing knowledge, engaging in a purposeful task that serves in a positive way the participants, the school program, the students, and ultimately the entire school-community. The true nature of the opportunities and challenges of school collaboration were expertly described by Pounder (1999, Fall) approximately two decades ago. Her article on the topic was set forth in an issue of the *UCEA Review* (see references). Contemporary leaders are encouraged to request a copy this issue from the UCEA headquarters. Current and past issues of UCEA publications and the SAGE Education collection are made available online to UCEA members at no charge through this portal. Pounder's article has said it best.

We keep in mind that collaboration has been recommended as a highly important consideration for fostering the effectiveness of contemporary education. In addition, it is included in most every prediction as a necessary skill for success in the future as well. The previously mentioned 1999 study by Pounder found that approximately 87 percent of the participating department chairs had specific collaborative activities between and/or among various state programs. Wide global network collaboration by school systems, however, has not yet been established by school districts to date.

Internal collaboration among students provides opportunities to foster leadership and to work cooperatively with others on difficult tasks. Students can assume the leadership role within the group and on occasion can take the leadership role as researcher, organizer, recorder, designer, or attend to other tasks facing the cooperative task group. Through their working on tasks collaboratively, other skills such as effective communication, judgment, problem solving, critical thinking, attention to details, and initiative come into play. Each of these skills remains important as one considers the skills needed for future success.

WHAT IS OFTEN OVERLOOKED?
A SNAPSHOT OF THE SMALL STUFF

In considering the knowledge and needed work skills necessary for future success, some of the "small stuff" frequently is overlooked. Of course, the characteristics of reliability, attention to work details, courtesy, responsibility, managing personal finances, and other such qualities are not so small when it comes to work-related success. These affective skills quite often are the causes of failure. Much more attention in contemporary educational programs must be centered on helping all students become able to take care of their personal matters. Being able to assume a positive place in society and to deal with the inevitable events of both success and failure are essential for fostering success in the worlds of today and tomorrow.

FAILURE IS ACCEPTABLE OR IS IT?

Let's set the standard for the high jump event in the boys' ninth-grade gym class to be 4'5". That is, to pass the class every student has to be able to jump at that height. In addition, every boy must be able to run the 100-yard dash in 15 seconds and be able to do 15 push-ups in order to get a passing grade in the class. At the start of the class, Delmar was able to clear a height of 3'5". At the end of the class and with considerable practice, Delmar was able to clear a height of 3'11". He finally lowered his 100-yard dash time to 15 seconds and was able to do 12 push-ups. On the basis of this record, Delmar failed the class standards. Delmar also failed pre-algebra. His pre-test score was 40 percent but his post-test score was only 60 percent whereby a passing grade was set at 70 percent. Delmar failed.

We stress the point that we are not speaking of the completely indifferent student who might be troubled by some inhibiting cause in health or family condition. The delinquent or laggard must be seriously attended by specialists who can help the student overcome his or her deficiency. Most everyone accepts the fact that students are different. Yet, expectations in terms of achievement commonly are set on the basis of standards that every student must meet. Students who do not meet the grade-standards in all too many cases are retained in grade or required to retake the course. The mark of failure is placed on the student, and a common answer for the student is to drop from school. Too much of an exaggeration? Just check the statistics. "Every year, 1.2 million students drop out of school in the U.S. alone" (DoSomething, no date, p. 1).

The learning success rate of each student must be identified, evaluated, and assessed and then be implemented in the learning plan of the student. Students are different. These differences must be understood if a positive learning culture in the school is to become a reality. Place the student at his success level rather than at his failing level. Yet, some failure can serve the student in a positive way.

FAILURE AS A POSITIVE HAPPENING

"Failure is the most important step to reaching success" (Allan, 2014, June 30). We contend that if you have never experienced failure, you probably haven't done much. Most everyone knows the history of failure related to Abraham Lincoln. President Lincoln experienced fourteen personal and political failures before being elected president of the United States. It looms important for students to know and understand the benefits of failure. Such a consideration tends to rail against the contemporary statements prevalent in many schools that failure is no option.

We understand that underlying meaning of the no failure statement. Every student should be learning at his or her ability level. However, students tend to view the statement as being more negative in that failing is not tolerated; one just has to succeed.

Yet, it is commonly known that everyone has faced or will face failure in life. Help students understand that failure is a common phenomenon. Failure can serve to help a person understand that the ability to survive can be enhanced. That is, failure provides each individual an opportunity to learn, to become stronger, and it should be looked upon as a benefit, and as an opportunity to build one's knowledge.

Winston Churchhill is reported to have said, "Success is the ability to go from one failure to another with no loss of enthusiasm." The ability to meet Churchill's contention may be difficult to accept. However, it does give each individual a chance to reverse the resulting feeling of being a complete loser and serves to place an emphasis on what that failure can do to provide opportunities to learn and improve.

A recommended activity following a failure or after completing the week at work is termed self-evaluation. Self-evaluation can serve as a growth activity for both students and adults. Take some time to be by yourself at home and focus on what communications and events took place during the week. Do some quiet thinking about the events that took place and the results that followed.

Give thought to the various activities and events that took place during the week. In each case, think seriously about the results of your activities and relationships with others. What went especially well and what did not seem to go well? Think about each question and the reasons that were in play regarding the positive and less positive outcomes. What did you do relative to each possible outcome? What might you have done differently and why? What improvements seem to be in order?

This form of self-evaluation reportedly has been a most beneficial self-development strategy for leaders that we have known. Personal development is closely related to self-development. Mentoring students relative to failure and how it can serve as a major growth opportunity is of paramount importance. Failure can be instrumental in helping students prepare for the challenges of tomorrow. Both adults and students can benefit by using some form of self-evaluation to examine the pluses and minuses that inevitably occur in one's life.

A LIGHTHOUSE EXPERIENCE: EDUCATION TECHNOLOGY

In the early 1950s a large black machine sat in the back of all the classrooms at the Lackland Air Base Instructors' School located in San Antonio, Texas. These "monster" machines, as they were called at the time, were never used because no one in the school or on the air base seemed to know what they were for. Sometime during 1950 to 1953, an airman named Paul Andereck discovered that they were a "giant" opaque projector purchased by the air force for instructional purposes at the instructors' school that trained air force teachers and conducted leadership development courses.

The large monster, of course, was a first model of an opaque projector and it allowed an instructor to project printed material or small objects onto a screen by placing the printed material or object into the projector and a bright light would shine on the material and the reflected light was directed through the projection lens. At the time, the opaque projector was a "revolutionary" instructional aide that most likely cost the air force thousands of dollars but went unused until Anderick's discovery. Paul Anderick, a noncommissioned airman, was flown around the country to various air force bases to demonstrate this new instructional technology. Andereck caught the attention of his air force member audiences by using a three-piece transparency that began with Marilyn Monroe fully clothed and ended with the famous Monroe calendar photo. At the early time of the 1950s, the "monster" overhead projector was viewed as a technical marvel.

THE THREE Ts OF TODAY'S EDUCATIONAL TECHNOLOGY

The three Ts of education in the years ahead are T, T, and T: *T*echnology as being commonplace in the classroom; *T*echnology as augmented reality for new student learning experiences; and *T*echnology for giving students more autonomy in deciding how they will pursue flexible learning assignments. The ongoing technological advancements today have developed so rapidly that teachers often "admit" that their students know more about computers and other communication devices than they do. Of course, teacher and administrator preparation programs necessarily must give technology advances special attention. In turn, local school districts must follow-up by having instructional development programs in the area of technology or the instructional staff will likely be unprepared to deal with the ongoing technological changes that are certain to take place.

NEW TERMS, NEW KNOWLEDGE, AND NEW UNDERSTANDINGS

In chapter 1, we were introduced a term that most likely was new for the majority of readers. *Neuroplasticity* is the agility of the brain to change. We learned that the brain is modifiable in the sense that human beings can continue to learn and create changes in their brains continuously. Check to see how many of the following terms may be new to you. Each term relates to the discussion of learning now and in the future.

Virtual learning, transparent communication, organizational silos, Socratic teaching, teacherpreneurism, MODUPOD, micro-credentialing, E-portfolios, mobile learning, open content, cloud computing, augmented reality, classroom gamification, stage-based learning, the Allosphere, and STEM knowledge are terms already 'in practice' or highly recommended for student learning. Improvements in educational improvements tend to follow technological advancements. We contend that improvements in education should be directly related to ongoing research that takes place at all levels of government and, of course, at the local school level.

A visit was made to a higher education program that was promoting the reimagination of education. Certain "new programs" such as open classrooms, on-site administrator training, and online programming were being emphasized. The question was asked about the foundations of the "innovation" and what research was in place to assess and evaluate the program's results. The response was that the program leaders were giving those questions some thought.

The primary purpose of chapter 3, as stated at the outset, was to examine the many predictions and current practices for preparing students for the decades ahead. The foregoing list of terms/practices gives some indication of this objective.

Virtual Learning—is the same or directly related to E-learning, web-based learning, online learning, distance learning, and blended learning. It consists of learning experiences that are facilitated through the use of computers and/or internal or external facilities of the school. Most frequently, virtual learning is online and therefore can be paced according to the individual's ability and environmental conditions.

Transparent Communication—Transparent communication generally is viewed as being important information that provides for the understanding at the time it is needed. It operates in an open climate whereby trust and honesty are fostered. Transparent communication is considered absolutely necessary for cultivating a positive climate in the school. It is viewed as being upward, downward, and horizontal within the system. As a result, trust is facilitated.

Organizational Silos—An organization silo is a close group of members that forms within the larger group of faculty members. Silos commonly are viewed as being negative since they do not want to collaborate with others within the system. Silo mentality reduces the ability to establish positive collaborative teams within the school or school system. Members of a silo group commonly work together but are uncooperative with others outside the group. Authorities set forth various ways to confront silos, one of which is to give major attention to improving communication within the entire school and school system. Silos tend to be the basic causes of problems within the school. That is why positive school climates must be enhanced by way of the development of schoolwide trust, collaborative relationships, and open communication for facilitating problem solving that must constantly be attended.

Socratic Teaching—Socratic teaching is a dated teaching strategy that emphasizes opportunities for the student to think critically. Rather than giving answers to student questions, for example, the teacher uses questions to respond to the student's questions. The strategy serves to lead students to new ideas that necessitate new thinking on the student's part. Some persons view the strategy as being cooperative argumentation whereby new probing results in new learning.

Teacherpreneurism—Teacherpreneurism is closely related to teachers who demonstrate high levels of innovation and creativity. Imagination is one characteristic that most commonly is associated with a teacher who is an educational expert, counselor, policy advocate, community organizer, and other tasks that serve to reform educational practices. The argument, of course, is that education needs more teacherpreneurs to work both inside and outside education to create better policy and programs for the benefit of student learners.

Mondopad—A mondopad is an all-in-one touch screen collaboration system for face-to-face collaboration with others in any location. It is reported to help teams work together for enhancing communication/collaboration. It is advertised as an essential tool for casting, whiteboarding, viewing documents, video conferencing, and more. We are reminded of the entry of the overhead projector into school audio-visual instruction a few decades ago. In a large school district in Lincoln, Nebraska, the central school district AV Center loaned its five or six overhead projectors to its twenty-eight elementary schools, four junior high schools, and four high schools. Over the years, sufficient funds made it possible to get at least one overhead projector for each school. Mondopods are expensive and will most likely be available to schools as time moves on and as monetary funds become more available. Then, too, mondopads will give way to new and more effective ways to carry out face-to-face collaboration anywhere at any time.

E-Portfolio—An E-portfolio is a collection of electronic evidence assembled and managed by a user usually on the web. It allows the student to collect, record, and assess their progress as related to a learning plan. E-portfolios play a significant part in a student's efforts to become a self-learner. The stored learning information provides many benefits including opportunities for self-evaluation, storing samples of completed work experiences, assessments of learning progress, special skill accomplishments, and examples of special creative projects that reveal such skills as critical thinking, innovation, and collaboration.

Micro-credentialing—Micro-credentialing centers on the efforts to recognize the accomplishments of workers by rewarding them a micro-credential or certificate of accreditation. It is commonly referred to as a mini-degree in some area of work that has resulted in a new skill or specialty for the employee. As such, micro-credentialing is a way for teachers to provide evidence of positive professional improvement relative to their position description. The medal or certificate is a way for the teacher to demonstrate their ongoing professional development and the areas of special skills in such areas as competency-based learning, student learning styles, decision-making, active styles of communication, listening skills, and other skill areas.

Mobile Learning—Mobile learning certainly is not new to most students today. It is education that is gained through the internet or network using personal mobile devices such as smartphones, tablets, or other electronic devices. Mobile learning is convenient for people who are on the move. It defies having students sit at a desk with only a pencil and paper in hand. Any handheld computer, MP3 players, mobile phones, and tablets are used and the strategy is viewed as being cost-effective and available from most anywhere at any time. Some sources have reported that mobile learners have added to their examination scores; learning has definitely been improved.

Open Content—Open content means that a publication or other document can be used freely without having to gain permission. It is said to have an open license. For example, someone can create something and let others copy or change it without having to ask permission. It serves to open the door for using more material for the major purpose of learning. This is most beneficial for the student in the development of his or her E-portfolio. Gaining permission to quote or use copyrighted material has tended to be more and more inconvenient. In some cases, the copyright owner charges a fee for the use of published material over the two-hundred-word free use principle.

The open content ruling opens the availability of other media such as texts, videos, pictures, and so forth. That is, the student can use the open content as he/she wishes. The material not only may be used freely, but it can be reproduced, edited, expanded, and republished as desired. Thus, learning sources are opened more widely for any and all learners.

Cloud Computing—Cloud computing, also termed on-demand computing, is a kind of internet-based computing that provides shared processing resources and data to computers and other devices on demand. It is the practice of using a network of remote servers hosted on the internet to store, manage, and process data rather than a local server or a personal computer.

As explained by Griffin (2016, June 19), "In the simplist terms, cloud computing means storing and assessing data and programs over the internet instead of your computer's hard drive." Cloud computing is predicted to become a part of school education programs nationally. Through the use of cloud computing, students are able to collaborate, store files, and utilize virtually many different applications in their education activities.

Classroom *Gamification*—Classroom gamification, interestingly enough, seems to come up on the pages of readings concerning the improvement of student learning at a surprising high level. The term *gamification* in education centers primarily on the process of transforming academic components into gaming themes. That is, it is viewed as literally creating a game out of learning by streaming all components of the classroom in a game metaphor making the classroom like one big game. In brief, the aim is to build games and reward systems around class activities and assignments. Supporters of the concept claim that gamification literally changed their classroom into an enjoyable learning environment. Students tended to "perk up" and participate actively in the gaming activities.

Gamification is not a complex and difficult concept. That is, it does not have to be so. Examples of gaming are giving points and keeping score of points earned for: (1) showing how a math problem could be solved in more than one way; (2) assigning student homework and test grades backwards (e.g., getting all ten answers correct is graded as zero; getting all answers incorrect is graded as 100 percent; getting six answers correct is graded as 40 percent). Other game points might be determined for wining a class game such as one invented by a middle school teacher in Nebraska.

MATCHO was a game related to the well-known game of Bingo. Each student had a MATCHO card with a variety of math problems on the squares. Various math problems that included fractions, percents, measurements, and the number system were on the various MATCHO cards. The teacher would draw a problem from the box of problems and say something like "Under M change 37.5 percent to a decimal." If the student had that problem on his or her MATCHO card, a chip was placed in that box. When any student has five problems in a row, they would call out "MATCHO." That student would then choose one of the five problems on the card to work out at the chalkboard. All other class members had to try to solve the problem at their desks. Students that got the correct answer received five points and the winning student would receive ten points for getting the problem correct. Each student would keep a personal score record for all points earned during each class game.

In another classroom game, a dartboard included fraction problems such as $3/4 \times 2/3$; $1\frac{1}{2} \times 5$; $7/8$ divided by 13; and $5\frac{1}{2} + 11\frac{2}{3}$; and $10 - 6\frac{2}{3}$. A bullseye automatically gave the student five points. The dart board commonly is magnetic and so darts are not steel pointed for reasons of safety. Whatever problem is hit by the student's dart must be worked out on the classroom chalkboard. All student participants win points for the record as per the requirements of the class. This upper-grade game was often played by students as a reward for achieving other class requirements.

More difficult activities, of course, can be used for games in advanced classes in most any other subject. In physical education activities, for example, basketball games, gymnastics, rope climbing, swimming, and other games are ideal for carrying out the intention of classroom gamification activities. In addition, teachers with whom we visited told us of gamesmanship activities that simply included points for having homework prepared and ready for checking the next day, having the high percent of students receive a grade of B or better on a class quiz or test, or having class teams consider a problem appropriate to the class subject and giving the best or most appropriate report on a matter that required critical thinking.

Stage-based Learning—Stage-based learning is the name given to the proposals that recommend the ending of age-based learning whereby students are placed in grades K–12 according to their ages and replacing that historical practice with placements based on how individual students were progressing academically. In short, students would be placed in school on the basis of their abilities to achieve. Those persons who recommend such a change argue that the present age-based system results in student disengagement from learning. High-performance learners reportedly become bored with material that they already know and perhaps are being "taught" for the second time. Slower learning students also tend to be disengaged since they need more time to learn the material at hand.

Other changes in stage-based learning methodology include the installing of a portfolio strategy for keeping track of achievement progress with a major reduction in the use of testing as a chief way of determining student progress. Strong arguments for stage-based learning also are set forth by the fact that many other positive learning opportunities become open to students who are working according to their individual interests and abilities. Self-development is made more possible and the qualities of critical thinking, creativity, and individual initiative are fostered.

The Allosphere—The Allosphere is a research facility located in California used to project computer-generated imagery and sounds. It is being mentioned here as an example of technological advancements that are certain to have major impacts on all matters to be faced in the future. Its potential for creating technology that will enable experts to use their intuition and experience to examine and interact with complex data in order to identify patterns, suggest and test theories in an integrated loop of discovery that would seem to open many new doors with implications for education in the future.

STEM—STEM is a well-known term for science, technology, engineering and mathematics. The term is used commonly when the topic of school curriculum comes to the floor. Science and mathematics have dominated the standardized testing era in America's K–12 schools. School curriculum has been directly influenced to the extent that advanced math courses that were taught previously in higher education are being offered at the high school level. For example, Calculus 101, years ago, was viewed as a "final" course for mathematics majors in most universities.

At present, precalculus and calculus 101 are common math courses in many high school programs. Although such change can be viewed as progress, it is noted here to demonstrate the influence of STEM on local school curriculum. Empirical evidence suggests that affective skills related to social behaviors are being projected as being of paramount importance now and for success in the future. Might the focus on social issues add an 'S' so that the term changes to STEMS?

A CHAPTER POST-QUIZ

Directions: For each of the ten statements, indicate whether it is primarily true or false.

1. Thoughts of gaining knowledge and skills outside and away from a physical classroom are being proposed more frequently by various "authorities." True____ or False____
2. When it comes to curricular program provisions, future predictions for school programs tend to be much more different than contemporary practices. True____ or False____
3. The future trends concerning work quality emphasize individualization as opposed to collaboration since better solutions come about when one person focuses on the problem at hand. True____ or False____
4. Workplace failure is viewed as being the number 1 problem of reaching future goals. True____ or False____
5. The organization silo is the practice of establishing best collaboration practices within the organization. True____ or False____
6. The term open content is the practice of establishing the best collaboration within the school. True____ or False____
7. Gamification in the classroom is viewed as one of the most troublesome practices that contemporary teachers have in place. True____ or False____
8. Stage-based learning is viewed as the practice of teachers standing in front of the classroom lecturing to their students who are sitting at their desks. True ____ or False____

9. Empirical evidence has shown that the physical environment in which learning is to take place has little or no bearing on achievement. True____ or False____
10. Most every practice set forth for education in the year 2030 has been supported by research in some manner by way of pilot programs and basic research. True____ or False____

ANSWERS TO THE CHAPTER POST-QUIZ

Statement #1 is *True*. Some "authorities" predict that contemporary classrooms and even schools will not exist in the years ahead. In any case, learning is not to be confined in any way to the closed-door classrooms that exist in schools today.

Statement #2 is *True*, although we count the answer of *False* correct as well. Some predictions go as far as to contend that school buildings and classrooms will not even exist in the future. Although most predictions contend that learning will take place within and externally to a contemporary school setting, most predictions center on open-door learning that includes learning being in place anywhere at anytime.

Statement #3 is *False*. Although individualization and self-development are noted as being of importance in the future, group collaboration is high on the list of future learning positives. In fact, collaborative arrangements among teacher groups and with others worldwide is given high marks for future learning by students in the years ahead.

Statement #4 is *False*. Some authorities have contended that failure not only will continue to be a factor within every organization, but that failure is a positive characteristic that promotes new thinking and positive changes within the school. That is, without failure, important improvements most likely would not take place.

Statement #5 is *False*. Silos are negative groups within schools that visit within themselves and shun other members who are not members of the silo. Silos interfere with the quality of effective collaboration that is required for developing the best educational program for students. Trust, cooperation, problem solving, and poor climate factors commonly are the results of silos within a school environment.

Statement #6 is *True*. Open content looms important for students and teacher who are seeking quality information for upgrading personal knowledge and skills. Open content does not require permission for its use in any way. Thus, students and teachers may use open content materials for their learning purposes without the red tape generally required when permission is required for its use.

Statement #7 is *False*. Gamification is a "fun factor" used by teachers to engage students in classroom learning and having them enjoy it. Creative strategies that bring humor into the classroom such as questioning techniques, jokes, games, contests, and role-playing are gamification examples commonly used by creative teachers.

Statement #8 is *False*. Stage-based learning is the opposite of age-based learning whereby students are "taught" and placed according to their age. Stage-based organization has students placed according to their current level of achievement.

Thus, students who are advanced in a subject are not caught in the waiting process while others in the class catch up. Thus, motivation is fostered on the part of the advanced learner while other students are moving at a slower but successful pace.

Statement #9 is *False*. Both empirical and basic research have shown that the physical environment in which learning takes place influences learning in various ways. Lighting, colors, physical arrangements, and climate factors influence student learning both positively and negatively. The point is that school personnel who work with students on site must gain more involvement in matters of school construction and school remodeling.

Statement #10 is *False*. Basic and empirical research are two factors missing from the large volume of future predictions for school operations. Educational research is the primary factor missing in the improvement of education nationally. The matter of educational research is considered additionally in the next chapter of the book. One of the most important yet unanswered question in education today is why research units do not exist in every school district or are not made available to every school district in the nation.

KEY CHAPTER IDEAS AND RECOMMENDATIONS

- Future predictions for the future of education in America as stated by various groups and individuals range from "much the same as today" to being "unbelievable." However, certain characteristics and skills such as collaboration, social skills, problem solving, and communication tend to be viewed as being of major importance today and in the decades ahead.
- Future predictions such as having schools with no grades, no examinations, and no teachers are among those future changes that are most difficult to imagine and perhaps to accept.
- The concept of stage-based education whereby there are no grades and students progress on the basis of their individual achievement does find support in many of the predictions that are set forth by various groups and individuals.

- Future predictions, such as "there will be no physical campus for schools, instead students will learn in traveling classrooms and the real world will be their campus," while fascinating, are most difficult to accept since no supportive operational information accompanies the contention.
- School construction assumes a more important need for school personnel involvement. Student learning environments are now viewed as being extremely influential in regard to enhancing student achievement.
- The lack of valid and reliable empirical and basic research in educational practices continues to be an inhibiting factor when attempting to determine today's curricular program and its relationship to the future success of students.
- Serious attention and research activities must be given to the effectiveness of future predictions such as the increasing practice of home schooling. To what extent, for example, are parents prepared to take charge of effective learning for their one or several children? What such training is available to parents even today? Teachers minimally take four years to prepare for teaching today. How are parents able to do this difficult task with no training whatsoever?
- The matter of educational finance support is seldom given major attention in discussions of education in the future. The "bland" statement that education must be supported falls short of answering the money questions. Increasing technological developments, worldwide education operations, and personal compensation all carry with them costs that will occur and payments that must be made.
- Teachers are not to be teaching but will become mentors and guidance persons. Just how teachers become mentors as opposed to teachers remains unanswered.
- The stated importance of collaboration rises high on the list of most important education needs and skills. Collaboration requires working together, meeting together, thinking together, and learning together. Distance learning does not seem to provide the closeness that is inferred by the skills of collaboration, empathy, communication, and other social skills. Our attention must be directed to just how we improve social relationships when virtual online relationships are dominant.
- Changes in educational practices most commonly are attributed to external technological changes and external mandates. How might education become the primary force that serves to determine the most relevant and effective changes that are needed to improve from the present stage to the next more improved stage of performance?
- Teacher and administrator preparation programs are in need of repair. Research in education is seldom viewed or stated as being of paramount importance for educational success now and in the future. We have it as being close to the number one need.

DISCUSSION QUESTIONS

1. Assume the role of Principal Doe who has been asked to speak to the local parent-teacher association on the topic, "Preparing Students for the Future." Think it over and then draft a page outline that sets forth the primary points that you will make in your twenty-minute remarks. Be as specific and informative as possible. Include your thinking on the topic relative to today's school programs and how they might lend each student information and skills expected for success in the next two decades.
2. Give thought to the curricular program of your school or one for which you are most familiar. List several curricular offerings and program activities that you believe are good examples of preparation of students for the future. Try to be specific in your response. Do not just list a course or activity that might be appropriate for fostering future success, but give evidence of just what knowledge and skills the school's program is definitely meeting this requirement.
3. Differentiate between age-curriculum and stage-curriculum practices. Explain each term to a friend, another teacher, or to a member of your family. In doing so, make note of their reaction to these curricular concepts.

REFERENCES

Allan, P. (2014, June 30). How to move past failure. *lifehaker*.
Blake-Plock, S. (2014, October 13). 21 things that will become obsolete in education by 2020. Learning, Innovation and Tech. The Daily Riff—Be Smarter About Education.
Bushmaker, T., Leed, A. P., and Koehler, R. (2015, July/August. School facility design for today and tomorrow. *School Business Affairs*. Facilities.
Dunwill, E. (2016, November 8). 4 changes that will shape the classroom of the future: Making e-education fully technological-Elearning industry. *Manufacturing Stories*. STEM Education. Dublin, NH 03444-0164.
Eisner, E. W. (2003–2004). Preparing for today and tomorrow. *Educational Leadership*. v. 6, no.4.
Fudin, S. (2011, November 15). What a classroom will look like in 10 years. *Main Menu*. University of Southern California, Los Angeles, California.
Griffin, D. (2016, June 19). Assignment IV-/Daniel Griffin Information. *Course Hero*. Columbia Southern U Business. BBA 2551 Homework Help. From the web: https://www.CourseHero.com/file/17590817/Daniel-Griffin-Assignment-IV/
Grzybowski, T. (2018). *The future of continuing education can be found in K–12 classrooms*. Madison, WI: Omnipress.
Hanover Research (2014). *How do we prepare today's learners for tomorrow's jobs?* District Administration Practice. From the web: HTTPS://ID.ISTE.ORG/CONNECTED/ISTE
Hoover Institution (no date). *American education in 2030*. An assessment by Hoover
Houshmand, K. (2018, May 11). Schools of 2030: No grades, no exams, no teachers? *The Globe and Mail Inc*. Toronto, ON, Canada, MSA ON1. Phillip Crawley, Publisher.
LAVA (2012, January 26). Classroom of the future by LAVA. *Archiscene*. Australia Education. From the web: https://www.archiscenel.net/education/classroom-future-lava/

McClure, R. (2016). Educational restructuring. *Creating the Future*. Compiled and edited by Dee Dickson. From the web: Archive.education.jdu.edu/PD/new/horizons/future/creating-the-future/cruft-mcclure.cfm

Pappafotopoulos, D. (2011, July 23). *Public schools for 2025: A vision for the future*. Educate Pleasanton Schools. Pleasanton *Commentary on the public schools in Pleasanton, CA*.

Pounder, D. G. (1999, Fall). Opportunities and challenges of school collaboration. *UCEA Review*, vol. XL, No. 3.

Willis, J. (2014, August 20). Preparing your students for the challenges of tomorrow. *Brain Based-Learning*. San Rafael, CA: George Lucas Educational Foundation.

Chapter Four

Education Today for Meeting the Challenges of Tomorrow

PRIMARY CHAPTER GOAL

To discuss what can be done in education today to prepare students for future success.

EDUCATIONAL SUCCESS TODAY AND
EDUCATIONAL SUCCESS TOMORROW

Previous chapters have focused on the condition of K–12 education today and the many predictions for education in the decades ahead. One thing appears to be true: although many changes will occur in the ongoing future, the affective and cognitive skills needed for success today appear to be highly necessary for future success as well. Future predictions for education have been stated by various individuals and study specialists in the fields of education, business, technology, science, and psychology. Chapter 4 centers on an analysis of the myriad of recommendations and predictions relative to the knowledge and skills that the student needs today in order to meet the needs of tomorrow. *Knowledge* is what the individual knows about something. *Skill* is determined on the basis of what a person can do.

Knowledge and skills needed in the future are of primary importance, but the characteristics of students, the physical arrangements/climate for student learning, and the education roles of students, teachers, and parents loom important as well. The purposes of education commonly center on two primary aims. One perspective is education's value for influencing the student's personal development by promoting individual autonomy, forming a personal identity, and establishing a career or occupation.

A second primary emphasis placed on educational purposes is vested in its contributions to societal purposes, including good citizenship, assuring the shaping of the individual into being a productive member of society, promoting society's free enterprise system, and preserving America's cultural values and foundational qualities of a democratic society (Winch & Gingell, 2008).

Attempts to meet the major purpose of chapter 4 require giving attention to the cognitive, interpersonal (affective), and intrapersonal skills discussed in each of the previous chapters. Keep in mind that the primary purpose is to discuss what is important for today's education to prepare students for success in the future. Those behaviors of importance are instilled in learners beginning at a very early stage.

The kindergarten students of 2018 will graduate from some form of secondary education in the year 2030. It seems most productive to examine ongoing trends to help project the knowledge and skills they will need. Present trends suggest that knowledge of technology and automation will be essential. The previously discussed cognitive skills of critical thinking, problem solving and creativity also are viewed as being crucial for success in the years ahead. Social skills center on abilities related to effective oral and written communication, collaboration, teamwork qualities, and problem-solving. Cooperation and teamwork now encompass the ability to work collaboratively with others within the local and global cultures. The matter of how the foregoing knowledge and skills are taught in contemporary programs must be addressed.

Collaborative learning in schools today is an interesting change from the longtime rule that the student must do his or her own work. Knowing a good way to resolve an existing problem and discussing the idea with a group of classmates are encouraged today. Group decision-making is welcomed. Good solutions and intelligent responses determined by a group lead to improved solutions and better practices.

SOCIAL SCIENCE LOOMS HIGH AMONG PROJECTED FUTURE SKILLS

The skills of being able to work together effectively is the sine qua non of collaboration and team workmanship. Respect remains imperative for success in the future. Chief executive officers have underscored the paramount importance of developing positive social skills including the characteristics of courtesy, respect, and willingness to work. Teachers in 2030 must have the capability of helping students develop strong social skills.

Recent survey results found that academic knowledge will not be the most important type of knowledge by 2030. In fact, the large majority of influential experts and practitioners at an annual summit in Dona were of the opinion that personal skills will be fundamentally important for success in the decades ahead (Mahaffie, 2014).

One might contend that social skills are "taught" via teacher modeling. Social skills can be developed through instruction and practice as well. Teachers are observed by students throughout the day. Politeness and other social skills are observed by students daily in the way that a new student is welcomed into the school; how visitors to the classroom are received; the comments of some student's positive words as they enter or leave the lunchroom table; or how a new substitute teacher is received by students. Along with modeling proper social skills, the teacher can create opportunities for students to practice and demonstrate positive social skills.

SOCIAL SKILLS CAN BE LEARNED, OBSERVED, AND PRACTICED

Virtually every statement of the "authorities" concerning student success in the future centers on the need for new skills. The question arises, however, as to what skills, affective or cognitive, are of most importance for meeting future needs. An affective skill is characterized by such behaviors as enthusiasm, creativity, compassion, communication, and kindness. Cognitive skills are abilities that are learned in varying degrees as an individual grows and develops; abilities that are used to learn, understand, and integrate information in a meaningful way. Memory, learning new information, understanding of information, and mental abilities are examples of cognitive skills.

THE IMPORTANCE OF AFFECTIVE SKILLS

In 2015, Norton set forth a list of thirty-seven affective skills that included enthusiasm, sense of responsibility, kindness, flexibility, compassion, high moral standards, creativity, patience, understanding, confidence, and others. A common affective skill listed by authorities is proactive behavior.

Proactive behavior, for example, is when the individual changes things in an intended direction for the better rather than fighting the fire trying to solve a problem after it occurs. Proactive behavior is related to adaptability, independency, and confidence. Such behavior is evidenced in having to face a mistake and the loss of confidence on the part of coworkers. Such leadership requires the effective characteristic of honesty which is evidenced by admitting a mistake and taking the responsibility for it. Such behavior can serve to mend relations and gain trust among the workers.

Nichols (2015, November 5) listed seven skills that students will always need: critical thinking, collaboration, agility and adaptability, initiative, effective oral and written communication, assessing and analyzing, and curiosity and imagination. Nichols viewed these skills as being of high importance for contemporary school programs as well as being those skills needed for future success. How are such skills brought to the attention of students?

On one occasion, for example, a speech and communications teacher took time to demonstrate how students should proceed with introductions of people. She underscored the importance of the student introducing his or her friend to a teacher. "Mrs. Hurst, this is my friend Betty Smith." The friend is presented to the higher authority who in this case is the teacher. The student who was introducing a friend to his mother would say, "Mother, this is my new friend, Sally Smith." That is, the individual is always presented to the person of higher authority or standing.

Another teacher took time to explain the difference between "pardon me" and "excuse me." She explained that "pardon me" was appropriate when one might step on another person's foot or when interrupting two persons who are in conversation. The polite words of "excuse me" are appropriate when one has to leave to answer the door or has to leave a meeting a few minutes early. The idea is the creation of opportunities for students to practice such social skills. Seems simple enough, but such skills must be practiced and learned.

Most every day a teacher is able to witness some act of social courtesy performed by students. A student greets a new student and directs or accompanies them to the next classroom. A student holds the school door open for another student or incoming teacher. A student excuses herself when leaving a table of students in the lunchroom. These social skills should be targeted and complimented by the teacher. On other occasions, poor social skills are demonstrated and intervention is needed. The teacher should meet the student who is involved privately and courteously "teach him or her" what was wrong and what should have been done.

However, socialization goes much deeper that just being polite. The term includes any learning that facilitates the interaction and communication with people. A course in Social Skills 101 would include the factors of coordination, mentoring, negotiation, persuasion, service orientation, and social perceptiveness. The characteristics of friendliness, participation, communication, and participation also are important social skills. We would add the proper use of the English language as an important social skill and we ain't kidding. Can I have your attention for just a moment? The following information is of great importance for he and she. Between he and I, there seems to be something wrong here. Please clarify the matter for Pat and I. Whoops! Indeed, something is wrong here.

The examples might be somewhat exaggerated, but one hears grammar mistakes being voiced by news reporters, sports announcers, and other TV personalities on a daily basis. The use of the words *may* and *can* commonly are misused as well. "Can I borrow your battery charger? My car won't start." Or, "May I borrow your battery charger? My car won't start." The word "may" is used as a courteous permission request while the word "can" expresses the ability to do something.

At certain times, articles on good social skills are available in the news or in book stores. Reading such articles and telling stories about courtesy and good manners can be memorable for students. Proper social skills at school events, school luncheons, guest presentations, and other activities hold many opportunities for students to be taught to practice proper social skills. Put students in charge of planning and carrying out arrangements for social affairs and certain school program activities. When students demonstrate the proper use of language or actions of courtesy, it should be recognized by the teacher.

Much ado about nothing? We do not think so. Neither do many knowledgeable individuals who have stated their opinions about education today and its implications for future success. As a CEO member of one study group noted, "CEOs argue that young people don't seem to have social graces and interpersonal skills such as respect. . . . They ought to have lifelong learning skills and to understand that learning happens all the time" (Dunwill, 2016, p. 18). While we look toward the future needs of students, attention to the proper social skills of today looms as being of high importance.

The predictions for the need of social skills in the future should not come as a surprise. Respect in today's world is wanting. We find incidences of disrespect at the highest levels of our government, in our business practices, in our homes, and in our schools. Nevertheless, virtually every prediction for a successful future has social skills high on the needs lists of managers within all organizations. The human element becomes a primary concern in the workplaces of the future. The concepts of collaboration and team working strategies lend additional credence to the belief that social skills will be highly important in the decades ahead. Helping students now to develop high levels of social demeanor is in need of major attention. But how do you teach them? Or, isn't this the parent's job? Yes, but the teacher must do for all children what the very best parents would do for their children.

Dana Truby (2013, October 1) has suggested that the social skills of listening, greeting others, asking for help, explaining how to disagree, demonstrating how to apologize, and explaining how to accept "no" for an answer can be taught through strategies of student engagement. For example, *listening skills* are enhanced by students practicing just what to do. Truby recommends that step 1 is to look at the person and remain quiet; step 2 is to wait until the other person is finished talking; and step 3 is to show that you have heard the speaker by nodding and using such phrases as "that's interesting," or "Okay." In such cases, the old adage that "practice makes perfect" applies.

Practicing listening is enhanced by having students tell each other about a recent vacation event or telling a joke or telling something about what they plan to do after graduation. The social skill of courtesy is also fostered in the way attention and politeness are exercised during conversational activities. The responses "Don, your vacation sounded like one that I would like to take sometime" or "Pat, I can't wait to tell that joke at the dinner table tonight" specifically indicate that Don and Pat were listening.

THE ENHANCEMENT OF SOCIAL SKILLS

Finding predictions for education by the year 2030 is not a problem. The problem is trying to summarize the myriad of predictions that are being proliferated. Various individuals, forums, survey results, authority assessment conferences, and a dozen other discussion groups have given their opinions as to what K–12 education will "look like" in the next decade. An opinion is commonly defined as a view or judgment about something, not necessarily based on fact or knowledge. It is a judgment, a viewpoint or statement that is not conclusive. In pursuing the matter of what skills are needed for success in the decades ahead, social skills are commonly included along with the need for new knowledge and skills.

It is beyond the scope of chapter 4 to attempt to detail all of the ways in which students can learn how to perfect social skills in a school setting. Thus, three important social skills have been selected for the purpose of demonstrating learning activities that center on socialization. For example, mentoring, negotiation, and service orientation are three social skills that are receiving more attention as the topic of future education in schools is examined. Although mentoring is being viewed as being increasingly important as a social skill, it should be viewed as an accomplice of collaboration as opposed to a new teaching strategy.

THE SOCIAL SKILL OF MENTORING: OLD WINE IN NEW BOTTLES

The social skill of mentoring certainly is not new to the education scene. Yet, both mentoring and reverse mentoring are commonly discussed when the topic of future education is on the table. Mentoring is a first cousin of the major social characteristic of collaboration. The practice of a teacher standing before a class of students dispensing information on some subject is being dismissed by most every presentation of future educational practices.

Rather, the "teacher" is to become a coach and/or mentor for students who are pursuing a curricular topic of personal interest. Mentoring or coaching as a development strategy for teachers has considerable potential.

A *mentor* is an individual who works cooperatively with a person within the profession.

A *coach*, on the other hand, can or cannot be a person in the same field as the individual who receives the services. Of course, the entire school staff works cooperatively in determining the purposes of the mentoring program. Just how the mentor and the protégé will work together and how the mentoring must be understood, how the members of the school faculty will be involved, and how the success of the program will be assessed are questions that are determined cooperatively by the parties involved.

The professional titles of school personnel or their time in service do not necessarily determine who serves as the mentor. Rather, mentor qualifications, commitment to the role, availability, listening skills, interpersonal relationships and experience are among the affective characteristics possessed by successful mentors. Cognitive characteristics of successful mentors include persons with results orientation, educational knowledge, a history of self-development planning expertise, well-known records of cooperative relationships with people.

Successful mentors are first to point out the personal benefits of serving as a mentor. They mention the benefits of having the opportunity to enhance their own careers, to learn along with their protégés, and to extend their own knowledge and skills. Thus, mentoring can serve as a powerful motivator for one's own professional advancement and job satisfaction. Successful coaching and mentoring demonstrate the positive applications of collaboration, critical thinking, problem solving, and human cooperation. Their extension in contemporary practice augurs well for their contribution to future success.

Reverse mentoring has become increasingly important in view of the fact that teachers in practice have been open in indicating that some students know more about certain technologies than they do themselves. The younger student, for example, is learning additionally while serving as the mentor for a teacher in the area of computer literacy or other areas of technology. Collaborative relationships are extended and cooperative working arrangements become a reality. Predictions for the future commonly place "teachers" in the position of being a guide for learning as opposed to a dispenser of learning. Mentoring and coaching exemplify the guidance conception. Telling and lecturing are replaced by questioning and listening. Then doing comes into play.

THE CHARACTERISTIC OF ADAPTABILITY: AN ESSENTIAL SKILL IN A CHANGING WORLD

Projections for the future make it clear that the knowledge and skills required for success are encircled by *symptoms of change*. The symptoms represent administrative tasks that must be attacked by implementing the primary reason why school administrators are hired, that of leading ongoing change. Such implementation requires the possession of both cognitive and affective skills. Collaboration, critical thinking, problem solving, and creativity are among the skills that are viewed as essential in today's world and will continue to loom important in the years ahead. The skill of *adaptability* must be added to the list. The ability to adjust to new conditions and situations is a required ingredient of organizational change; without it one's success is severely limited. It has been said that adaptability cannot be taught, it must be learned.

The individual with high adaptability easily adjusts to new priorities, activities, and his or her own attitudes to meet new school targets and/or deadlines. The one with effective adaptability finds ways to accept daily changes that inevitably occur, finds ways to make things work, is acceptable to learn new ways to do the work and accepts new challenges and is open to change in order to be successful in a new environment or in meeting work adjustments. Adaptability becomes of vital importance because it is necessary if the student is to be successful in a world of change.

The old adage, "But that's how we've always done it" is the road to failure. Life is constantly changing to meet the needs of a changing world. Contemporary education programs must include program experiences that serve to help students adapt to changing situations, improve the situations, and overcome the troublesome conditions being faced. Adaptability is served by providing learning experiences such as the ones that follow.

Adaptability #1

A student in grade 3 was involved in a serious accident. The student was not wearing a seat belt. When his mother turned a sharp corner, he fell from his seat in the car into the street. The student was scratched and bruised and suffered a broken right arm. The student did return to school within the week but could not write with his right hand and thus had to use his left hand. The teacher, Anna Jenkins, gave thought to an adaptability matter. Might it be an interesting learning lesson to have all of the third-grade students write only with their left hands? Interestingly enough, other students thought that this change might be "kind of fun" and went along with the change. In short, the change only lasted for one week but the students did not seem to think the change back to the right hand was "just great." In fact, some students continued to use their left hands for some writing activities. Some students, on the playground, tried using their left hand in batting practice and shooting baskets. Of course, none of the students became left handed, but their dexterity with their left hands improved in most cases and the experiment was talked about for a long time. The point here, of course, is vested in the experience as being a lesson in adaptability.

Adaptability #2

A junior high school student (Monte Scott) was also a member of the school's track team. He ran both the low and high hurdle events and commonly come in second in both events at the regularly scheduled track meets. At the time, running the high hurdle event was a 110-yard event and the low hurdles was a 220-yard event that required running the early part of the race on a curve. Scott went over each hurdle with his right foot first.

At one time during the mid-season, the track coach asked Scott about taking the hurdles with is left foot rather than his right. The left-foot strategy would give him some advantage when running the curves. Monte practiced the left-foot strategy for two weeks and increased his event time enough to qualify for both the high and low hurdles at the statewide track meet. His adaptability helped him to win second place in both the high and low hurdles with best times in each event.

The foregoing adaptability stories are not presented as best examples, but rather as examples of what a creative teacher can do to encourage adaptability in their students. The "we've always done it that way" thinking leaves no room for improvements or creative changes to mediocre practices. Giving students opportunities to resolve the problem, find a more effective way of doing something, or finding a way to "bounce back" from a disappointing performance are most likely to be possible through increasing the student's adaptability. Most likely there is not a course available on the topic, but opportunities for fostering the skill exist in every school program activity.

ATTENTION TO DETAILS: A SKILL OF PARAMOUNT IMPORTANCE FOR FUTURE SUCCESS

We contacted several individuals in the various fields of business and asked them about knowledge and skills that they viewed as being of great importance for future success. This contact was not viewed as a valid research effort but rather as an informal visit or telephone call with managers, officers, and CEOs in practice. The general responses of digital skills, social skills, collaboration, problem solving, and accountability were common but the skill of "attention to details" represented a brief unique response that gave thought for examination.

We searched for an answer to the question, "What is so important about giving attention to details as a success factor in the future?" Attention to detail, according to the responses given by business leaders, is viewed as the gold medal of professional workmanship, quality, and reliability within the business world. How does one improve this skill? *Get Organized* was the number one response.

Organizational Development was a major topic of discussion earlier in chapter 2. Getting organized includes such "obvious" practices as using a monthly calendar to note appointments, deadlines, and forthcoming dates of importance. Making lists of events, meetings, and contacts serves in determining priorities and preparing for effective participation. Make note of what you want to accomplish by each activity. What key information do you hope to gain and what few questions will keep you aware of the major purposes and specific details that must be attended?

One of the primary components of Organizational Development is that of planning. Planning serves to give serious attention to purposes. Purposes provide an opportunity to give thought to who we are and whom we serve. What must be done to meet these goals and objectives? In the teaching of reading, attention to detail is critical for accuracy. It is necessary to focus on the details of the word. Focusing on accuracy, pronouncing every sound in the word, placing an emphasis on accuracy as opposed to speed, and giving special attention to detail serve the student in many ways for paying attention to details.

If you already have a strategy for limiting distractions, have it copyrighted. There are positive suggestions for developing attention to detail and school programs must give special attention to them. Attention to detail is often misunderstood in business. It doesn't mean that a person is without great ideas and plans. Paying attention to details can derail a problem and result in giving an organization a reputation of reliability and professionalism. It must be viewed as a vital component of success.

HELPING STUDENTS DEVELOP THE SKILL OF BEING ATTENTIVE TO DETAILS

We relied on an article by Gagen (2008) as an example of using certain techniques for teaching/developing attention to details. She emphasizes the point that developing the ability to carefully and accurately pronounce all of the letters/sounds in a word is helping the student develop such skill. Think about the words detract and detach, addition and addiction, flow and flew, loose and lose, turkey and turnkey, from and form, and bother and brother. The letter *t* is pronounced specifically in the words after, it, teacher, and master. However, the letter *t* is silent in the word often. This detail must be stressed in classes as often as it is misused; detail is facilitated.

NEGOTIATIONS AS A POSITIVE ACTIVITY: ARE YOU SERIOUS?

In the early 1960s, relationships among and between the school districts' administrative and teacher staffs were not on the best terms. Teacher groups were at the table bargaining for higher salaries, more power, and less work. At least, that was the picture of collective bargaining from the view of the administrative staff. During this time in education's history, teacher sit-ins and strikes were at an all-time high. High-powered negative negotiations were the closest that teacher and administrator groups came close to any collaboration practices. Negotiations tamed a bit as the years went by and the term collective bargaining was changed to collective negotiations and then again to professional negotiations. Most every state passed legislation that approved the practice of teachers negotiating for salary, benefits, and conditions of work.

Today, professional negotiations are viewed as being "the way of life" although occasional teacher walkouts and strikes still take place. Negotiators on both sides of the practice are more experienced and prepared to serve as a negotiator for their party. Give-and-take agreements are considered and determined today and most all parties tend to agree that the negotiation activities will continue in the years ahead but not without some major differences.

NEGOTIATIONS WILL CONTINUE TO BE A PART OF OUR EVERYDAY LIFE

It doesn't take much thought to realize that negotiating is a common practice in most everyone's daily life. Negotiation looms important since it helps problem solving, reaching mutual agreements, and getting what is needed in our everyday lives. Coming to grips with the selling price of a new car, working out a new position description for a new course in social science, deciding on a new system for student grading at the elementary school level, or deciding on the request received by a local club's vocal group to use the school's music room after school hours all involve the implementation of some form of bargaining.

Reaching agreements on the use of certain instructional resources, deciding the guiding rules and regulations for off-campus instructional programs, and implementing a new student council program in the school all require getting "yes" responses from other individuals or agencies. Negotiation is defined as: "a back and forth communication designed to reach an agreement when you and the other side have some interests that are shared and others that are opposed. When two or more persons have a similar interest, but have some differences relative to governmental controls or purposes, they meet and confer."

Developing the needed skills cannot be viewed as a once-in-a-while activity for some students. Rather, the development of skills such as attention to details and negotiations must be included in the curriculum appropriately from kindergarten to grade 12 or as they fit the case.

Every curricular offering provides opportunities for learning activities that enhance the student's knowledge and skills in the broad areas of communication and collaboration. One skill that is often overlooked is *service orientation*.

SERVICE ORIENTATION AND FUTURE SUCCESS

Most every job or activity that an individual engages in today involves meeting and communication with others. When such contacts are not done with some sense of service orientation, problems as opposed to progress are likely to result. *Service orientation* is viewed as the ability of an individual to recognize and meet the needs of others. Service-oriented individuals take positive steps in making themselves available to others, sometimes even before the needs become most serious.

Service orientation becomes important not only for being helpful, thoughtful, and considerate of others, but also for the projected importance of collaboration, cooperation, teamwork, group decision-making, and other cognitive and affective skills. In view of the ongoing concern of low academic achievements on the part of students, that are greatly influenced by the condition of a service orientation culture within the organization.

Being aware of the needs of others centers on the quality of the interaction that takes place in social settings. Authorities have stated that positive service orientation within an organization underscores the achievement of success. When the "soft skills" of listening, understanding, empathy, and caring cannot help or resolve a matter, the skills of mediation, negotiation, and critical problem solving are available. Service orientation, as stated previously, is more of a school culture than an activity. Think of the many ways is which service orientation can be fostered in schools. Special cases are addressed as follows:

- Donald was highly handicapped physically and speaking. He could not walk and used a large wheelchair to move from place to place. He loved football, so the students in the school made certain to go to the home of Donald and take him to all of the home football games. The local school

team won the last game of the season and with it also won the conference championship. The team members each signed the game football and presented it to Donald as the team's "best fan." Few can forget how well this action was received by Donald.
- Young Richard fell from the back of his dad's pickup and was seriously injured. He was not able to return to school for several weeks. Classmates had a bed-desk made for him in the school shop so that he could read and write while in bed.
- The Hessons had an acreage of ten acres about seven miles from the school where their son, Henry, went to elementary school. Henry's father became ill and was short of help doing the errands at the acreage that included the picking of potatoes in a large half-acre field. One of Henry's classmates mentioned the need of help in one class session and six classmate volunteers walked to the acreage one Saturday and spent the day digging and picking the potato crop.
- The ninth-grade students at Roosevelt Jr. High School set up a tutoring service for those who needed special help with homework assignments. The service was available for one hour each day after school. The volunteer tutors were required to maintain a personal B grade average for service as a tutor. Tutors received no pay. Each tutor was required to send a letter to the parents that explained the purpose of the tutoring service and asking their permission for the service to be rendered. A teacher-sponsor supervised the tutoring service making sure that the homework service was a learning activity.
- In the high school class of Civics 1, a unit on service orientation was designed and implemented. The civics teacher led the completion of an instructional guide for the course with student representatives serving on the curriculum guide committee. The guide set forth the concept that service orientation was more than a process; rather it centered on the concept that being helpful, thoughtful, considerate, and cooperative was the foundation of positive relationships that served the climate of the high school. Being of service to others was viewed as the foundation for success.

The terms cooperation, collaboration, communication, and coordination all infer a condition of relating in a positive way with other individuals and groups. When predicting characteristics and qualities needed for future success, the four Cs of cooperation, collaboration, communication, and coordination are commonly listed as being of paramount importance. The characteristic of *coordination* reportedly was first recorded in 1595–1605. The term is most often defined as the organization of the different elements of a complex body or activity so as to enable them to work together.

The scientific management concepts of Frederick Taylor swept the industrial organizations from 1911 to the early 1920s with the requirements of the task system that ruled on control and efficiency. Each worker's job was specifically stated and controlled by the shop manager.

The following era of human relations was ushered in by Mary Parker Follett and others who focused on the concept that organizations were people and the concept of "power with" as opposed to "power over" was the answer to organizational success. That is, organizations are people and people are the ones who determine the success or failure of an organization. The concept of coordination was important for bringing the harmony in human relationships that could be established by identifying common elements in groups of workers.

THE IMPORTANT QUALITY OF COORDINATION

The concept of coordination was revolutionary when set forth by Mary Parker Follett in 1924. Follett's four views of coordination were set forth in her book *Creative Experience*. Horizontal as well as vertical coordination were to be in practice through direct contact by the workers. At the time when policy matters were being decided, coordination among personnel was viewed as being essential. All factors of a situation were to be considered in any situation with attention being given to their effects on these factors. In addition, coordination was to be viewed as being a continuing process. Decisions within the organization were to be determined with the combined knowledge and skills within the organization; coordination was to be considered as a dual responsibility of management and workers (Follett, 1924).

The human relations era and coordination brought about new thinking relative to the importance of the workers, their ability to cooperate, the need for positive collaboration, the paramount importance of open communication, and the importance of other affective skills such as service orientation and worker job satisfaction.

There is little question that such social skills will continue to be valued for success in the years ahead. Many of these skills can be modeled by parents at home and teachers in the classroom. Courses and program activities today must give serious attention to the practice of such skills in school programs. Reports of student violence, early dropouts, lack of respect and other positive civil behaviors must be seriously considered in each and every course and program activity that the school provides. Civics classes, home economic classes, social studies classes, business classes, and others provide learning opportunities for students in the areas of social skills.

It is quite likely that student graduates in 2030 will be working with an increasingly diverse work population. The need to be able to work cooperatively and in a collaborative and social-emotional way with colleagues looms important for success. It is clear that jobs of today require a variety of cognitive and social skills. High school graduates of 2030 will need to have knowledge and skills that enable them to work with cross-cultures. Lifelong learning, as previously noted, becomes the education purpose for success in the future. Complex problem solving, communication, collaboration, adaptability, attention to details, cultural sensitivity, and social-emotional intelligence are included in the compilation of knowledge and skills that should be programmed in 2019–2020 for success in the year 2030.

TECHNOLOGY AND FUTURE STUDENT SUCCESS

The ability to use technology and assume the position of continuous learning will be necessary for future success. Without question, skills that enable students to use technology will be of utmost importance for a successful career. As stated by Paul Peterson in an article by the Hoover Institution (2019), by 2030, "Courts and collective bargaining agreements will also gain in influence. Meanwhile, high school graduation rates will fall and learning will stagnate. Fortunately, those trends will be disrupted by an enormous rate of change in curriculum design and information dissemination made possible by technological innovation" (p. 1).

Caron (2011) and other authorities have focused on the matter regarding what students need to be successful in tomorrow's workforce. Caron points to several "missing links" concerning skills needed in the future. The importance of effective communication has been emphasized throughout the chapters of this book. Caron agrees. She notes that since more and more work is done by teams of people around the world—face to face and virtually— culturally sensitive communication takes on a greater importance than any time previously. In addition, Caron points out the many benefits of failure. This topic was discussed in-depth earlier in chapter 3.

STEM (science, technology, engineering, and mathematics) is viewed as a continuing need for future success. As stated by Caron (2011), "Clearly, science, technology, engineering and mathematics are and will be the drivers of innovation. Innovation is vital to the country's economic growth" (p. 1). Give some thought to how education today can be developed in students today. One teacher told us that she asked her students to consider what they would do to improve their e-phones or desk computers. Their answers were fascinating. For example, one student mentioned the continued improvements of 3-D imaging as it might apply to medical practices, building construction, archeological investigations, and underwater exploration.

POST-QUIZ FOR CHAPTER 4

1. Which entry below best describes an E-Portfolio?

    a. a collection of electronic evidence assembled and managed by a user on the web.
    b. any message that is sent or received on a computer or i-Phone.
    c. the entry job description for any clerical work that can be redefined easily by electronics.
    d. the same thing as a T-Portfolio only it is used most commonly by entry or new teachers.
    e. a running record of the ongoing use of electricity assumed by electronic devices used in school classrooms.

2. Check each of the strategies that follow that center on improving a worker's attention to details:

    a. limit distractions
    b. get organized
    c. avoid overworking your brain by taking regular breaks
    d. make lists and enter "to do" items on the calendar
    e. encourage accuracy over speed of completion

3. high school graduates of 2030 will likely find themselves:

    a. involved in jobs of specialty whereby working alone gives one more authority.
    b. working with others whereby social skills take on increasing importance.
    c. having to make more and more individual decisions regarding problems encountered in the workplace.
    d. working to develop a full set of cognitive skills; social skills tend to take care of themselves.
    e. in the classroom after school doing homework in school rather than at home.

4. Which entry below is mostly unlikely to exist? The layout of classrooms in the decades ahead will:

    a. look much the same as they did in 2019.
    b. have standing desks for students who have difficulty maintaining attention while sitting.

c. have moving walls that will make more spaces more adjustable.
   d. have private work stations to accommodate the completion of individual tasks and collaborative work spaces for group projects.
   e. have special lighting that facilitates student attention and learning.

5. According to most every future prediction, education in the future:

   a. will be much the same as in 2019, except the school year will be extended by at least sixty days.
   b. will witness the transition of the educational model whereby many of the contemporary jobs will still be present and only the technological devices in schools will be more evident.
   c. will see education change from a teaching to a learning model whereby new roles for teachers will be mentors and coaches.
   d. will simply include the contemporary curriculum but will be made more available to students online or by other forms of delivery.
   e. will be determined exclusively by the agencies of the federal government, which will assume 75 percent of the necessary funding for K–12 education.

6. Surveys and other individual and group predictions for education in the future commonly predict that:

   a. online content will become the number one most important source of knowledge.
   b. teachers of tomorrow will be much the same as teachers of today and will be the primary source of learning data for students in grades K–12.
   c. local school control of K–12 will disappear and the federal government will assume control of curriculum and funding.
   d. although technology will change production efforts in industries around the world, it will not impact so profoundly on education since it is a learning phenomenon and not a business industrial matter.
   e. the matter of the value/benefit of technology for education is still to be determined. To date, sufficient research has yet to be developed that demonstrates the real effect of technology on student learning.

7. The question, "What are the critical challenges and how is the school teaching agility, adaptability, and resilience?" is one that needs to be addressed by schools to determine:

   a. if the student is gaining sufficient knowledge and skills for school graduation.
   b. if the cognitive skills have been learned by students who are to graduate.
   c. how the school faculty is preparing their students to respond to the future skills needed in the workforces.
   d. students' affective work skills.
   e. all of the above.

8. STEM is the acronym that stands for:

   a. Student, Teacher, Education, Model.
   b. School Team Educational Model.
   c. System Teaching and Education Mastery.
   d. Temperament Traits for Employment Maintenance.
   e. Science, Technology, Engineering, Mathematics.

9. Clear communication is not just a matter of proper use of grammar and language, but it is definitely an extension of:

   a. clear thinking.
   b. being heard.
   c. being adaptable.
   d. social standing.
   e. a person's IQ.

10. Stage-based learning is:

    a. when the teacher stands in front of the students serving as the disseminator of knowledge.
    b. when the teacher has planned the lesson for the day with little or no opportunities for any changes in methods or strategies.
    c. when the lesson for the class today includes a quick review of yesterday's class lesson for purposes of continuity.
    d. based on the learning status of the student rather than the age or grade of the individual student.
    e. none of the above.

ANSWERS TO THE POST-QUIZ

1. The answer to question #1 is "a," an E-Portfolio is a collection of electronic evidence assembled by a user on the web. It is a compilation in digital form used for evaluating course work and/or assessing the student's achievement.
2. The answers to question #2 are "a," "b," "c," "d," and "e." Each entry serves the purpose of helping the individual to pay closer attention to details. For example, getting organized commonly is the first recommendation set forth by authorities for helping persons to increase their ability to pay attention to details. Failure to do so can result in additional problems that are costly to the organization.
3. The answer to question #3 is "b," working with others whereby social skills become of high importance. Previous concepts of having a student work alone and doing his or her own work have been changing toward the concept of needed collaboration, and group results tend to be of higher quality than individual decision alone. Not only will collaboration be promoted in the learning activities in the classroom but communication with others in the school district, the states and the world is expected to be increased in the decades ahead.
4. The answer to question #4 is "a" stating that classrooms of tomorrow will be much the same as today. Some predictions contend that student learning will take place in a variety of settings and that the contemporary classroom is unlikely to exist. Open education whereby students are learning outside a campus setting or contemporary classroom is a common prediction. That is, student learning will take place wherever they may be; self-education is to be prominent.
5. The answer to question #5 is "c," whereby education will assume a learning model as opposed to a teaching model. In doing so, teachers will become mentors and coaches as opposed to disseminators of information. This prediction is common among the many predictions for the future of education. If such a prediction actually occurs, the term teacher reasonably would disappear. One new term that has been used to identify the new roles of teachers is that of teacherpreneurism. An entreprereneurial teacher is first and foremost an imaginative teacher. He or she is a risk-taker in regard to methods and strategies for engaging students in learning activities.
6. The answer to question #6 is "a" regarding the importance of online learning. However, answer "e" has merit as well. Although online learning has been well established in educational practices today, it seems certain that its presence will increase in the decades ahead. Valid and reliable research activities are needed to address the question of student achievement. What have been the major academic

outcomes of online teaching to date? Is convenience, outreaching, extensive programming and cost factors enough to replace face-to-face teaching/learning as we have known it?
7. The answer to #7 is "e" since each of the possible responses have some merit in response to the question as to whether schools are teaching and students learning the affective and cognitive skills that are needed now and for future success.
8. The answer to #8 is "e." STEM is Science, Technology, Engineering, and Mathematics. However, we are reminded of the recommendation that the letter S be added to the acronym since social issues are viewed as being of high importance for success in the decades ahead.
9. The answer to question #9 is "a," clear thinking. Clear thinking becomes necessary not only for effective communication but is crucial for effective problem solving, decision-making, collaboration, and giving attention to details.
10. The answer to question #10 is "d." Stage-based learning is offered in opposition of age-based learning. Age-based learning includes the continuation of placing students in grades K–12 in the same classrooms according to age. Commonly, for example, all students at the age of five enter kindergarten. At age six, students move upward to first-grade and so on. On the other hand, stage-based learning places students in various courses and learning activities on the bases of their stage in the learning process. Academic growth and readiness determine the courses in which a student will be placed.

YOUR POST-QUIZ RESULTS

10–9 correct ***** You are ready to move on to Norton's forthcoming book, *Educational Theories and Their Effects on Contemporary Program Practices.*

8–7 correct **** You deserve the chance to read Norton's 2018 book on *Dealing with Change: The Effects of Organizational Development on Contemporary Practices.*

6–5 correct *** You qualify to read Norton's 2019 book, *Making Our Schools the Best in the World: Re-Imagining Education Outside the Proverbial Box.*

4–3 correct ** Norton's book, *The Changing Landscape of School Leadership* focuses on educational change and how to deal with change today. You would find it of special interest.

2–0 correct * You might benefit considerably by rereading Norton's 2019 book, *Today Is Tomorrow.* Be sure to take each pre- and post-quiz that is included in some chapters. Pay close attention to the details of each paragraph of each chapter.

KEY CHAPTER IDEAS AND RECOMMENDATIONS

- The affective and cognitive skills needed for success today appear to be highly necessary for success in the years ahead.
- The focus on students doing their school work alone is receiving attention. Collaboration is moving into the picture whereby teamwork and collaboration are being viewed as a positive position change.
- Although technological knowledge and skills are necessary for success today and are looked upon as highly essential for success tomorrow, social skills are being viewed as the sine qua non of successful practice in the future.
- Coaching and mentoring are being predicted as being the primary responsibilities of teachers in the future. Stage-based learning is the new kid on the block. Students will move ahead in learning at the time that they are prepared to do so; age-based learning is losing ground in education.
- Adaptability, attention to detail, negotiations, and service orientation are on the list of skills that will be needed for a successful work life in the years ahead.
- The ability to use technology and the position of continuous learning will be the path to follow for future success.
- Science, Technology, Engineering, and Mathematics (STEM) are viewed as important today and will continue to be necessary for success in the future. Although it is clear that no one has the key to the door that tells us what knowledge and skills will actually be needed in the decades ahead, historical and contemporary evidence tends to reveal that technical skills remain as essential for future success.

ACTION ACTIVITIES

1. Divide the students in a class or perhaps persons who are in attendance at a faculty party into groups of four to six persons. Have them discuss the question: "How can our after-school activities be improved?" Give each group appropriate time to discuss the question. Have each group present their results. Have the group combine similar ideas. Place the final ideas on a chart and have all members rate each entry as first choice, second choice, third choice, and so forth. Have the group as a whole discuss how the final choice or choices will be implemented.
2. Chapter 4 discussed the concept of teachers working as coaches and mentors. Consider the matter of implementing such program proce-

dures. What kinds of preparation would most likely be necessary? How would a school program a mentor/student plan including such matters as how students are assigned to mentors, how many students would be assigned to a mentor, and when and where does the mentoring take place?
3. Assume that you are a member of the high school's engineering class. Your final semester exam included a question as to what you believe you would be doing ten years after high school graduation and what skills would you have to have for a successful work life. Write a page as your answer to the question posed.
4. Give consideration to the teacher preparation program commonly in place in universities today. Consider what changes, if any, you would program for individuals just entering the teacher preparation program. Be specific in your response. List specific skills to be developed and course activities that you will recommend.
5. We have used the phrase, "Today is tomorrow," through chapter 2. You have been asked to speak at a parent/teacher event on the topic of "How are we preparing students today for success tomorrow?" Take time to draft your outline for the remarks that you plan to present.

REFERENCES

Caron, S. W. (2011). Tomorrow's workforce: What students need. *Education World.*
Dunwill, E. (2016). 4 changes that will shape the classroom of the future: Making education fully technological. *eLearning Industry.* From the web: https://elearningindustry.com/4-changes-will-shape-classroom-of-the-future-making-education-fully-technological
Follett, M. P. (1924). *Creative experience.* New York: Longmans, Green.
Gagen, M. (2008). Developing attention to detail when reading: Key points, information, and techniques. From the web: https://www.righttrackreading.com/keypointsattention.html
Gingell, J., & Winch, C. (2008). *Philosophy of Education.* London and New York: Taylor & Francis Publications.
Hoover Institution (2019). American education in 2030: An assessment by Hoover Institution's Koret Task Force on K–12 education. Stanford University.
Mahaffie, J. B. (2014, September 15). Nine skills that will help make our children future-ready. Qatar Foundation: Doah, Qatar.
Nichols, J. R. (2015, November 5). 7 skills students will always need. *teachthought.* From the web: https://www.teachthought.com/the-future-of-learning/how-to-prepare-student-for-21st-century-survival/
Norton, M. S. (2015). *Teachers with the magic: Great teachers change students' lives.* Lanham, MD: Rowman & Littlefield.
Truby, D. (2013, October 1). 8 social skills students need (and how to teach them step by step!). *We Are Teachers.* From the web: https://www.weareteachers.com/8-social-skills-students-need-and-how-to-teach-them-step-by-step-2/

About the Author

Dr. M. Scott Norton has served as a secondary school teacher of mathematics, coordinator of curriculum for the Lincoln, Nebraska, School District, assistant superintendent for instruction, and superintendent of schools in Salina, Kansas, before joining the University of Nebraska as professor and vice-chair of the Department of Educational Administration and Supervision. Later he served as professor and chair of the Department of Educational Administration and Policy Studies at Arizona State University where he is currently professor emeritus.

His primary research and instruction areas include educational leadership, human resources administration, teaching methods, governance policy, the assistant school principalship, competency-based administration, the school principalship, research methods, organizational development, organizational change, organizational development, organizational climate, and educational program improvement. He has published widely in national journals in the areas of teaching/instructional methods, organizational climate, gifted student programs, great teachers, student retention, organizational change, and others. He has published widely on a variety of educational topics for the Rowman & Littlefield Publishing Group.

Dr. Norton has received several state and national awards honoring his services and contributions to the field of education and educational administration, including awards from the American Association of School Administrators, the University Council for Educational Administration, the Arizona School Administrators Association, the Nebraska School Administrators Association, the Arizona Educational Research Association, Arizona State College of Education Dean's Award for Distinguished Service to the Field, and the Arizona Information Service, and the award for service as president of the College of Education Faculty Association. He presently is serving as a member of the Arizona State University Emeritus College.

Dr. Norton's state and national leadership positions have included service as executive director of the Nebraska Association of School Administrators, member of the board of directors for the Nebraska Congress of Parents and Teachers, president of the Nebraska Council of Teachers of Mathematics, president of the Arizona School Administrators Higher Education Division, and member of the Arizona School Administrators' board of directors, staff associate for the University Council for Educational Administration, treasurer of the University Council for School Administration, state representative for the Nebraska Association of Secondary School Principals, member of the board of editors for the American Association of School Public Relations, and council member for the Arizona State University Emeritus Council.

www.ingramcontent.com/pod-product-compliance
Lightning Source LLC
Chambersburg PA
CBHW030147240426
43672CB00005B/299